UNCERTAIN JUSTICE

Fixing the Problems with the Police, Prisons, Immigrants, Opioids, and the Divisions in America

by Paul Brakke

Author of:

Crime in America,
Fractured America
Fixing the U.S. Criminal Justice System,
The Price of Justice in America,
The Costly U.S. Prison System,
and
Cops Aren't Such Bad Guys,

UNCERTAIN JUSTICE

Copyright © 2019 by Paul Brakke

ACKNOWLEDGMENTS

I am indebted to Gini Graham Scott for much help in the writing and preparation of this book. Further, I would like to acknowledge the assistance of publicist Jana Collins. My thanks as well to Christin O'Leary for her help with the social media, Alinka Rutkowska for her insights on book launches and promotion, and Gus Sandi for his work on creating the American Leadership Books website. Additionally, I want to thank QuickGraphic99 of 99design for designing the cover for this and my previous book *Crime in America.*

TABLE OF CONTENTS

INTRODUCTION: WAYS TO FIX A CRIMINAL JUSTICE SYSTEM IN CRISIS

Considering How to Fix the Criminal Justice System

Today, the criminal justice system is in crisis. U.S. prisons and jails are overcrowded with over 2.2 million convicts, and people are increasingly scared by the number of mass murders in America. They have good reason to be scared, given that the recent Thousand Oaks shooting massacre was the 307th *mass shooting in the US* in 2018 -- an average of over one a day. And the shootings continue in 2019.

That's why I'm continuing to comment on recent events in my latest books *Crime in America* and *Fractured America,* and my forthcoming *Prisons in America.* And that's why I have combined my ongoing commentary on the system into this book *Uncertain Justice.* In these books, I have considered what's wrong with the current system for dealing with crime in America and provide suggestions for what to do.

All of these books and my everyday commentary are written from a conservative perspective, describing some fixes to make the system more efficient and cost effective. I have also been suggesting ways to reduce crime and recidivism with community based recommendations to help individuals become more productive citizens and preserve family unity. This way, individuals have less incentive to return to crime and end up back in prison.

Most of the other books on the criminal justice system are written from a liberal perspective, based on bringing a social welfare perspective to crime and punishment. The emphasis is on supporting individuals who are hurt by an unjust system and therefore providing them with funds and mental health treatment. The liberal approach also tries to get defendants a reduced punishment by citing the way they have been disadvantaged by their poor income or conflict in their family. The claim is that the many institutions in society have abandoned them, so let's help.

The problem with that liberal approach is the criminals who are helped in this way often see such as a greenlight to offend again. By contrast, the conservative approach takes into account the safety and security of the community, too, and seeks to help them become more productive citizens who have less incentive to return to crime as a result. This approach doesn't deny them treatment or assistance by the community, but the goal is to provide them an alternative to returning to their criminal ways, not provide them with a "poor me" excuse to get them a lighter sentence if they return to crime.

So it is in that spirit that I have been expressing my comments on what is happening in the arena of criminal justice and the divisions in society that are tearing America apart. Initially, these comments have been expressed in a series of press releases. Then, after nearly three months of sending out these releases, it seemed like a good time to collect the current series together into a book. In the future, as I continue to post and send out releases, I'll plan to collect another series of commentaries into another book in the future.

The Beginnings of Uncertain Justice

Uncertain Justice was born after I, assisted by my marketing and publicity assistants Gini Graham Scott and Jana Collins, began posting a series of news releases in response to the events of the day involving crime, criminal justice, or divisions in American society. I also commented on the latest conflicts involving the police, the courts, immigration, and the opioid crisis.

In the process, I drew on the material I had written about in my seven books, including *Crime in America, Fractured America, Fixing the U.S. Criminal Justice System*, and others. But now I applied these ideas to the day to day news about these topics.

Initially, I just posted occasionally, beginning in December 2018, but then I began to post and send out these releases a few times a week. Eventually, I had nearly 30 of them, and I decided to compile my thoughts about these events into a book.

While the releases were written like a journalist describing my observations, research results, and quotes by me, I have converted them here into a series of first-person written chapters, in which I comment on these issues, divided into these sections:
- Improving citizen-police relationships
- Promoting prison reform and better prison sentencing
- Healing the divisions in American society
- Dealing with illegal immigration
- Dealing with the opioid crisis
- Portraying the criminal justice crisis in popular culture.
- Using a social media and video campaign to help fix the criminal justice system

The last section describes how I have been using a series of daily social media posts five times a week and over four dozen videos to get out the message. Six months of these posts are featured in *Crime in American in a Nutshell,* while the videos are posted on my YouTube channel for American Leadership Books.

So join me to read my latest thoughts about what's happening with crime, criminal justice, and the divisions in America, and how to fix what's wrong with them.

I

PART 1: WHAT TO DO ABOUT CITIZEN-POLICE RELATIONSHIPS

CHAPTER 1: HOW CITIZEN POLICE ACADEMIES AND COMMUNITY POLICING CAN REDUCE COMMUNITY PROTESTS AND PROPERTY CRIMES

Citizen-police relations have become tenser than ever. Every news cycle brings more examples of deteriorating relationships. For example, in the inner cities, protests are growing in response to police killings of civilians, even if an officer is cleared due to acting in self-defense. At the same time, property crimes are increasing and going unsolved in middle and upper income areas in the cities and suburbs.

It's a situation that is more and more untenable and we have to fix it. For example, still another protest occurred in Alabama, after a police officer was cleared of wrongfully killing E.J. Bradford, following a shooting at a shopping mall in the Birmingham suburb of Hoover. The officer mistook Bradford to be the gunman, since Bradford was running with a handgun drawn in the crowded mall, and the officer thought he might hurt others, so he was justified in shooting. But the protesters blamed the officer and showed their distrust of the police through their protest.

Meanwhile, an epidemic of car break-ins and other property crimes has infected many cities around America. These crimes even resulted in a senator in California, Scott Wiener, introducing a bill to enable prosecutors to better prosecute such crimes by not having to prove a car's doors were locked to get such a conviction, as described in an L.A. Times article in November 2018, "'Epidemic' of Car Break-Ins Prompts California Bill to Assist Prosecutions" by Patrick McGreevy.

While the two situations are very different, I see common links in the decline of community trust in the police in different types of communities. On the one hand, lower-income individuals don't trust the police because of racial profiling and the many cases in which the police have killed black males due to their fear they pose a threat rather than trying to defuse the situation with less lethal means. On the other hand, middle and upper-income individuals don't trust the police to deal with the rise of property crimes. That's because the police don't have either the time to investigate them or the ability to find the criminals, who are often a part of an organized crime group that is reselling their property on the black market.

A similar approach could be used to improve citizen-police relations in both communities, though the particular tactics might differ. Through such means, we can find ways to promote better citizen-police understanding and trust, and two ways to do this are through community policing and educating citizens through a citizen-police academy. In turn, the police will better understand the needs and wants of the citizens in the community where they are policing.

This idea of community policy has a long history, dating back to 1967, when President Lyndon B. Johnson appointed a Blue Ribbon committee to study the distrust of the police by many community members, especially in the black community. The resulting report by the President's Commission on Law

Enforcement and Administration of Justice suggested developing a new type of police officer to act as a community liaison and work on creating a bridge between law enforcement and minority community members.

The basic way community policing works is to assign officers to a specific area or beat, so they become familiar with the community, and then design specific patrol strategies to deal with the kinds of crimes that occur on the beat. For example, officers might seek to have an increased community presence to prevent criminal activity rather than respond to it. They can also solve problems raised by members of the community and promote positive interactions with the police anytime they are on patrol in the area or respond to a request for assistance. This community policing approach can work both in low-income minority communities and in middle and upper-income communities by adapting to the different types of crime problems in each community."

Some of the different methods include:

- having crime prevention meetings to provide advice on what to do, from protecting against inner-city gang violence to protecting one's home or car in the suburbs against a burglary,

- giving talks at schools and community centers,

- helping citizens create neighborhood watch groups and speaking to these groups,

- increasing patrols on foot, bicycle, or scooter rather than driving around in a car,

- partnering with other organizations, such as nonprofit service providers, private businesses, and the media,

- decentralizing police decision-making, so lower-ranking officers have more discretion.

The growing use of technology by police forces around the nation can also help to increase police effectiveness in many ways, from using cameras to record police activities to more quickly pinpointing the location of a crime. However, since this technology can reduce direct citizen-police contact, the police need to use community policing to promote further citizen-police interaction and understanding.

The Center for Evidence Based Crime Policy calls community policing "the best known and certainly the most widely adopted police innovation of the past three decades." In fact, recent research suggests that "close to 100 percent of larger agencies claim to have adopted community policing."

To this end, one program that many departments have adopted and I recommend is offering a Citizen Policy Academy (CPA) to help improve community relationships. The CPA does this by helping participants better understand "the procedures, responsibilities, demands, and laws that officers face," as Chief Rob Hall points out in a post on PoliceOne.com. Further Hall suggests that "a CPA is a unique and powerful means to increase the community's empathy and sympathy for law enforcement officers. It provides an opportunity to humanize law enforcement officers, to get to know the actual person behind the badge."

There is even a Citizens Police Academy in my hometown in Little Rock. It gives citizens an inside look at the Little Rock Police Department's policies and personnel. Much like these academies in other cities, the Little Rock CPA is held once a week for eight weeks and covers a different area of the police department each week. It's taught by certified police officers, supervisors, and personnel who are knowledgeable about a particular division.

Typically, CPAs cover these topics: the department's organization and ethics, an overview of the legal system, procedures on the use of force, firearms training, traffic/DWI enforcement, forensics, and recruiting. The academies usually offer jail tours and ride-alongs, and some include SWAT and K-9 demonstrations. There is even a National Citizens Police Academy Association with member police departments around the U.S.

We now need these programs more than ever, given these growing conflicts between police and citizens in the inner cities and the growing fear of crime throughout the country. The

16

particular community doesn't matter, because these programs can be adapted to the needs of citizens in each area. What is critical for the program's success is encouraging increased personal relationships between the police and members of the community as part of an effort to prevent crime and protect the community. The police shouldn't just be there to respond after a crime has been committed.

CHAPTER 2: THE REFLECTION OF U.S. DIVISIONS IN CONVICTING A CHICAGO POLICE OFFICER FOR A KILLING

Was Chicago white police officer Jason Van Dyke guilty of killing black teenager Laquan McDonald, when he believed the teen was threatening him with a knife? If he was guilty, was the sentence of six years and nine months enough? And did three other officers in the Chicago police force conspire to cover-up video evidence in the deadly shooting?

These were among the questions being asked after Van Dyke received his less than seven year sentence and the three officers were acquitted. Pedictably the verdict inspired protests from local activists who considered the sentence a slap on the wrist, believing that Van Dyke should have been given a much longer term.

In turn, the debate over this trial and that of other police officers accused of killing black citizens reflects the deep divide in American society between different racial, ethnic, economic, and other groups. As a result, even the actual facts of the case became subject to dispute.

The McDonald case is a perfect reflection of the different views of the facts of what happened. It also illustrates the differing views of an appropriate penalty held by members of these opposing divisions. That's because of their predispositions to view both the facts and penalty for a guilty verdict in a different way.

Black Americans and liberals are predisposed to view the cops as hiding behind the cover of their position to use racial profiling to judge blacks on the streets as likely suspects in a recent crime. So they think the police are ready to shoot to kill based on imagining the suspects pose an immediate danger, even when that's not the case. By contrast, whites and conservatives are more likely to see the police as justified in these shootings, because the police are often facing dangerous criminals and are tasked with keeping the community safe, so conservatives feel they are normally justified if they have a reasonable fear of their life. As a result, most whites and conservatives will believe an officer's statement of being in fear of his or her life.

Accordingly, the McDonald trial and verdict are perfect examples of how these different perceptions of the police shaped the opposing views of the trial and the results. For example, whites and conservatives believed, along with the jurors, that Van Dyke truly believed that McDonald was advancing towards him brandishing a knife. That's why the jurors ultimately found Van Dyke guilty of manslaughter, but not murder. By contrast, the blacks and liberals who protested the results believed that the video of the shooting did not show McDonald actually threatening him. However, it could be that a video taken from another angle or at a different time would show that McDonald did present a threat.

Likewise, the response to the verdict shows this split. On the one hand, those holding a conservative view believed that Van Dyke should have been found not guilty or at least be given a much shorter sentence. Van Dyke's wife expressed this conservative view when she stated, "My husband does not deserve a lengthy sentence for doing his job as a police officer."

On the other hand, the blacks and other protesters holding a liberal view felt the verdict and sentence should have been much harsher. For example, from their perspective, Van Dyke should have been charged with murder, and he should have gotten a much longer sentence. In their view, expressed by one local activist, Van Dyke got a slap on the wrist because "People want Jason Van Dyke to do virtual life in prison…Anything less would not be justice for Laquan McDonald."

This kind of division in viewing both the evidence in the case and the verdict is reflected in most cases of the police killing blacks. That's why it is difficult for the defendant to get a fair trial or for people on both sides to feel satisfied with the verdict. I wrote about such divisions in *Fractured America,* which describes the many ways in which America is divided not only by race and political attitudes, but by ethnicity, geography, income inequality, generations, and more. At one time America was seen as becoming a melting pot, but in fact, that has become less and less true, and we are being broken up into lots of little pieces.

It is also important not to use the conviction of one officer for using inappropriate force in killing a citizen to tarnish the reputation of the police generally, although liberals often do this, using the actions of one to undermine the reputations of the many. In other words, if a police officer is ultimately convicted of homicide or manslaughter in a particular killing or has been charged with and convicted of misconduct, this shouldn't sully the reputations of the vast number of police officers who are diligently doing their jobs.

So what is the solution for these divisions in viewing a case? I recommend that the leaders of these different groups need to come together and discuss how to seek common ground and find ways to look at the facts more dispassionately. This way there can be a mutually agreed upon way to deal with these cases that involves all members of the community, not just the perspective of one side or the other. It is a way to come together around a mutually agreed upon approach, rather than further inflame differences.

CHAPTER 3: HOW POLICE DEATHS BY CITIZENS ARE IGNORED DUE TO FOCUS ON THE CRIMINAL

Both the media and citizens have been overly quick to find the police at fault about some cases where citizens have been killed by the police. Similarly, the media and many citizens have been quick to blame illegal immigrants as a group when one of them kills a police officer. But demonizing a whole group -- cops in the one case, illegal immigrants in the other -- by the behavior of one individual is wrong.

Then too, a police officer can be falsely portrayed as a criminal killer when the officer kills a suspect in the line of duty. The police officer's justification for the killing is commonly ignored due to an emphasis on the unfairness of the system, usually toward minorities. Instead, the focus should be on getting the facts, as I have discussed in more detail in chapters on the police and on dealing with illegal immigrants in *Crime in America.*

For example, in many of the high profile cases of a citizen killed by the police, such as in the killing of Trayvon Martin in Florida, Freddie Gray in Baltimore, and Eric Garner in New York

City, the protests and sometimes riots have portrayed the police as engaged in unjustified criminal acts. Later, the protesters have accused the justice system of being corrupt when the police involved in these killings were subsequently found not guilty of murder. However, the statistics present a different story, since 99% of the police officers involved in killing 1165 people in 2018 were not charged with a crime. A key reason is that the police are largely confronting hardened criminals who have just committed crimes, are trying to evade police capture, or are threatening the police. In these cases, a killing is justified as the appropriate use of force.

As for the cases of cops killed by a few illegal immigrants, most recently the killing of California Police officer Ronil Singh on December 26 by Gustavo Perez Arriaga, this is one of the few cases of an illegal immigrant killing a police office. By contrast, far more officers are killed by American citizens. But such details are ignored when these cases are used to make political points. Instead, the outrage should be over the high number of on-duty police officer deaths which surged to 140 in 2018, up from 129 in 2017, including 5 officers who were ambushed and killed in 2018.

Thus, we need to look at the overall statistics as well as hard facts in a case, rather than using an individual incident to paint the police as the bad guys.

PART 2: WHAT TO DO ABOUT PRISON REFORM TO REDUCE INCARCERATION, RECIDIVISM, AND CRIME

CHAPTER 4: HOW GIVING A NEW ANTI-OVERDOSE DRUG TO INMATES CAN HELP EX-CONS ADJUST TO LIFE AND REDUCE CRIME

Drugs and drug-overdoses have long been a problem in prisons, since according to some estimates, as many as 85% of prisoners are incarcerated due to crimes related to their use or sale of drugs. In fact, the rates of opioid and all types of substance use disorder are much, much higher behind bars than outside, according to addiction medicine specialist Dr. Sarah Wakeman of Massachusetts General in an August 30, 2018 interview on "All Things Considered,"

She described a wonderful new approach in many U.S. prisons to provide inmates with medication for opioid use disorders or to give anti-overdose drugs to inmates leaving prisons.

It's an effective way to treat substance abuse in prisoners and to help inmates being released avoid a return to drugs.

In one of the examples in Rhode Island, which has a $2 million state-supported program, every new prisoner in the correctional system is screened for opioid addiction. Then, those who need it are given medication assisted treatment (MAT), which includes the drugs methadone, buprenorphine, or naltrexone. Additionally, the correctional system established 12 community-based Centers of Excellence to continue the MAT therapy and provide support to prisoners once released. The therapy and follow-up support have proven effective, since there was a 60% reduction in overdose deaths in the first six months of the program.

Unfortunately, this approach is still rare in the nation's prisons, since most offer no medication-assisted treatment. But over 400,000 prisoners, 20% of the nation's 2.3 million inmates incarcerated for drug offenses, might benefit, as might even more inmates using drugs in prison -- estimated at about 25% of the prison population. It also helps any inmates with a history of addiction to go on a drug program with methadone, Suboxone, or Vivitrol at least a few months before their release, because just-released former inmates have the highest risk of dying from an overdose. That higher risk is because ex-cons who haven't been using drugs in prison are more vulnerable to overdose on smaller amount of drugs. Those who have been using in prison, which might well be most prisoners, probably are equally vulnerable to overdose as users on the outside if they take too much of the drug. In addition, besides taking the drugs, they should have the support of a peer-recovery program and better prescription monitoring.

Another good approach to reducing overdoses is giving at-risk inmates the overdose-reversing drug naloxone to take when they or those around them think they could be in trouble. The drug can even be administered with a nasal device. That's what's being done in Alameda County in California, in Chicago, in New Mexico, and in other cities, counties, and states around the U.S. For instance, in December 2018, Alameda began offering at-risk inmates the drug upon their release, and 56 of 78 at risk departing inmates took the prison system up on the offer.

Given the success of these programs, they should be expanded throughout the United States. These programs are also consistent with President Trump's opioid initiative, announced in March 2018. This initiative pledges to screen all federal inmates for opioid addiction when they enter prison and to facilitate Vivitrol treatment if they are released to residential community centers. In addition, the initiative calls for increased federal support for state and local drug courts to provide treatment to addicted offenders.

Thus, there should now be federal funds to support the program, and all states should pass their own legislation and funding for such programs to cut down on addiction and overdose deaths of both prisoners and ex-cons. Then, too, prisoners might voluntarily participate in experimental treatments to test their effectiveness and safety before bringing them to the general public. Prisoners who volunteer could have their sentence time reduce, thereby giving prisoners an incentive to volunteer.

CHAPTER 5: HOW PRISON REFORM EFFORTS HAVE CONTRIBUTED TO DECLINING HOMICIDE RATES

Declines in homicides in big cities have been reported nationally, according to the U.S. Department of Justice, and one factor contributing to this has been criminal justice reform. Such reforms are much needed, as I have discussed in more detail in my latest book, *Crime in America* from American Leadership Books.

One of the most important reforms is reducing incarceration sentences for prisoners convicted of less serious nonviolent crimes. This key reform not only reduces costs but it returns prisoners to their families and communities. The result is they are less likely to return to crime, thereby reducing recidivism rates, and more likely to become productive citizens -- a win-win for the individual, the criminal justice system, and the American economy.

A good example of the connection of this wider reduction in homicide rates and prison reform is a recent report from the San Francisco Bay Area, where homicide rates in San Jose, Oakland,

and San Francisco dropped by 26% over the past two years -- from 199 in 2016 to 141 in 2018. While one reason for the drop has been law enforcement's focus on gangs, illegal firearms, and the worst criminal offenders, another reason is criminal justice reforms, which include shrinking the prison population. This decline in incarceration occurred with one proposition -- Proposition 47-- which lowered some low-level felonies to misdemeanors, and another -- Proposition 57 -- which provided more chances of parole for nonviolent offenders.

In *Crime in America,* I have discussed the importance of prison reform and reducing sentences for non-violent less serious offenders at more length. This discussion includes extensive statistics showing the relationship between reduced incarceration, lower recidivism, and rehabilitation and treatment for prisoners and ex-cons. In addition, I provide many other suggestions for better ways to improve relationships with the police and deal with the opioid crisis and illegal immigration. Other chapters in the book discuss finding ways to create safer communities with less conflict between different groups in society based on race, ethnicity, income, and other differences. And now I am reaching out to legislators and governors to consult with them on the best approaches to criminal justice reform in their jurisdiction.

Such reforms are desperately needed because we need to make changes based on current data about what works and what doesn't. We should learn from other countries, too -- especially about the more effective prison policies in countries like Germany, Sweden, and Norway, which emphasize rehabilitation, shorter sentences, and getting ex-cons who have committed less serious crimes back into the community, so they can unite with their families and become more productive citizens.

CHAPTER 6: HOW REDUCING RECIDIVISM CAN REDUCE MASS KILLINGS

In the first few months of 2019, there have been over 300 mass killings, and the usual liberal response is to call for reducing the number of guns. The kids from Parkland High School have contributed to this call for gun control and to the drumbeat in the media to get rid of guns.

However, there is another more effective way to reduce the number of mass murders in America - one advocated by many conservatives who don't feel gun control is the answer. Rather they view most mass murders as due to a mental illness, given that most of these murderers are loners who have trouble relating to others in their school or community. Some killers also have a pattern of past violence and brushes with the law, or they have been in and out of rehab facilities or mental hospitals.

Accordingly, one way to better deal with the problem is to reach out to individuals who show signs of being an alienated loner to help integrate them back into the community and turn them into productive citizens. This is also a way to reduce recidivism and the high cost of incarcerating prisoners who have committed minor non-violent crimes. That is because over-incarcerating prisoners not only increases costs, but it contributes to the crime rate, since it leads to the break-up of families and makes it more difficult for ex-cons to get jobs. Instead, it is better to find ways to reintegrate ex-cons into the community and help them find jobs.

The same principle might be applied to individuals who are at risk of becoming the next mass murderer. An effort might be made to identify individuals, especially males, who are loners and seem to be either closed off from others or acting out aggressively. Identifying them will allow professionals to help such loners get reconnected to others. All it might take is reaching out to them like a friend to dissuade them from acting on their anger by shooting others they feel wronged them or randomly picking off victims. It doesn't matter whether they are seething internally or are acting out like bullies. The same strategy of offering them friendship and community support might work to keep them from killing others.

The advantage of this approach is it provides a community-based solution to help individuals become more productive citizens, preserve family unity, and create stronger communities. This way, with closer more cohesive communities, supportive friends, and jobs, individuals have less incentive to return to any type of crime, including committing a mass murder. The strategy helps ex-cons avoid returning to prison, and it could similarly help to keep prospective mass murderers from killing anyone.

CHAPTER 7: THE VALUE OF GETTING A GED OR HIGH SCHOOL DIPLOMA IN PRISON

In many prisons, inmates now have a chance to get a GED (General Equivalency Diploma) or high school diploma, and such programs can contribute to turning prisoners into productive citizens. This can thereby reduce recidivism and the crime rate, as I have described at more length in my latest books with a chapter on prison conditions, *Crime in America,* and in my forthcoming *Prisons in America.*

This chance to get a GED or diploma in prison is crucial, because about 70% of all inmates never graduated from high school, and these programs give them a chance to get either a GED or high school diploma. Having this degree plays a major part in getting hired for a job and opens the door to further education and better jobs and business opportunities in the future.

An example of these successful programs is the Lockhart Correctional Facility, a minimum-security women's prison in Central Texas. The prison has one of the high school programs in

Texas prisons. After the inmates leave prison, teachers at the prison help the ex-cons find jobs.

Such programs help reduce costs of imprisonment and recidivism, contribute to a reduction in crime, and strengthen families by helping prisoners get the skills they need to better get a job when they come out. As a result, they are less apt to return to crime. A reason these programs are so valuable is that about 70% of American prisoners have not completed high school, though they need that diploma to get many jobs.

Minimally, they should get a GED, which is equivalent to a high school diploma, although it is not equal, since it only teaches prisoners the basic reading, comprehension, writing, and math skills. It doesn't offer classes on specific subjects, such as history or geography, so the prisoner who gets a GED doesn't learn all of the subjects someone would take in a regular high school. At least it helps in getting a job upon release, and it opens the door to getting a higher education after prison.

Getting this education is really important for prisoners who haven't graduated from high school, since education offers an opportunity for social and economic mobility after their release from prison. This education also saves the state and nation a huge pot of money, because most of these ex-cons go straight when they leave with a degree that helps them get a job and reconnect with their family. Then, they have much less incentive to return to crime once they are working again.

A good example of this cost savings is what the state of Maryland spends on education and incarceration. It costs around $12,000 per year per public school student from K-12. It costs only $45 more for the students to take the four sections of the GED. But the state spends around $37,000 a year for each person they incarcerate - about three times as much. In Arkansas the state spends $800-900 per year to educate an inmate, while an inmate who returns after a release costs the state about $25,000. This education reduces the odds the prisoner will return. Just think how much the state could save by putting this money into helping prisoners get a high school or GED degree, so there would be fewer incarcerated individuals, due to less recidivism as a result of less crime.

Thus, it makes economic sense to provide a GED or high school education for those who don't have either. For instance, a 2016 RAND Corporation study found that individuals who participated in any kind of educational program while in prison were 43% less likely to return to prison. Plus other research has consistently shown the benefits of getting an education in prison -- among them an increased personal income, lower unemployment, greater political involvement and volunteerism, and better health.

The big reason for these differences is being better able to get a job after prison. Ex-cons with a limited education often find they don't have financial resources or a social support system after they get out of prison. Consequently, they are more likely to commit a criminal act rather than becoming reintegrated into their community. Financial numbers show the need for this high school GED education even more, since taxpayers will generally save four to five dollars that would be spent on incarceration for every dollar they spend on prison education. Those statistics come from a March 2018 article on "Educating Opportunities in Prison Are the Key to Reducing Crime" published by the Center for American Progress.

Finally, another social benefit occurs in that since ex-cons are more likely to be employed, they pay more in taxes and have more purchasing power. Moreover, by becoming self-sufficient citizens, they are less reliant on government programs. So it's a win-win for both the individual and society. For example, Missouri saved approximately $25,000 per year for every incarcerated individual who didn't return to prison. Thus, if a high school diploma or GED can help to keep released inmates from returning to prison, let's go for it. Let's provide the funding to make these programs happen.

CHAPTER 8: SHOULD PRISONERS BE ENTITLED TO FREE COLLEGE?

FROM STATE OR FEDERAL FUNDING?

Should prisoners be entitled to free college? Does this really make sense? Despite my endorsement of GED programs for prisoners, my answer is a very firm "No!"

Free college programs for prisoners are now being offered in a growing numbers of states. It's an approach described in a recent article, "State Partnering Colleges with Prisons. U.S. Experiment Studies Learning's Effect on Inmates," by Stephen Simpson, published in the *Arkansas Democrat Gazette*. The article describes a program at Shorter College in North Little Rock which instructs inmates from the Arkansas Department of Corrections at Wrightsville. After two years, these convicts receive an Associate of Arts degree, as they might at a junior college.

The program has even gained support from Arkansas Governor Hutchinson and Senator Boozman, who both attended a graduation ceremony and were very enthusiastic about the program. Even so, such a program is overly expensive and not appropriate for government funding.

By contrast, there are a number of problems with a college program. First, the big problem with state or federal funding for criminals in college is that those places could be taken by other students who would be paying tuition. Why should criminals get a break and obtain a free college education unavailable to law-abiding citizens? Moreover, very few prisoners qualify for such a program. About 70% lack high school degrees, and the vast majority of prisoners are poorly educated and some are nearly illiterate. Therefore, getting a high school diploma or its GED equivalent makes much more sense, since this would help ex-cons get jobs upon release, and all citizens are entitled to a free public education through high school. In fact, GED instruction is required in state prisons in Arkansas.

But a college education normally requires a paid tuition. Accordingly, such college education programs shouldn't be provided for prisoners by the state or U.S. government, since the U.S. already has a nationwide college loan debt crisis. Rather, any funds for education should go to ameliorate that debt, not to provide these funds for college for criminals in prison.

A related reason for not funding these college-for-prisoner programs is that colleges should work on increasing their own graduation rates, not offering programs to prison inmates. For example, Shorter College, cited in the article, is an African American private two year junior college with a graduation rate of only 9% within three years. Unfortunately, most of the vast majority of students who don't graduate within 3 years -- 90% of them -- will be stuck with a student loan debt for the rest of their lives. That's an average cost of about $18,000 for three years for tuition, fees, books, and supplies -- and all for nothing.

While most other universities don't have such a high drop-out rate, many other colleges and universities, whether state or private, have graduation rates in the 20 to 30% range. That means that 70 to 80% of their students without degrees nevertheless ended up with high student loans they still have to pay off at exorbitantly high interest rates. The borrowers can't even discharge these loans in a bankruptcy. So this is another crisis better addressed by state and federal funds rather than investing in college for criminals. Additionally, why keep colleges open that fail to educate most of their students? Instead, many colleges with low graduation rates should be closed, even if they are the only higher education institutions that serve their rural communities. Students in those towns who sincerely want a higher education should go or commute to nearby cities for their higher education.

Finally, the low unemployment rate all across the nation is one more reason why funding college tuition for prison inmates is not the way to go. Because of this low unemployment rate, employers are already having a hard time filling their positions, so the need for a college degree for a small number of ex-felons is minimal. Rather, any funding should go to help these employers find employees, perhaps by providing funds to train recently released ex-cons with high school diplomas or GEDs on how to find jobs. Then, when these ex-cons are better equipped to find jobs, that will add more prospective employees to the jobs pool. Additionally, some funds might be provided for jobs training, so the ex-cons can work in those fields where employers need employees.

PART 3: FIXING INJUSTICE IN PRISON SENTENCING - THE PASSAGE OF THE FIRST STEP SENTENCE REFORM BILL

CHAPTER 9: THE FIRST MAJOR
REWRITE OF SENTENCING LAWS

Now that the Senate has overwhelmingly passed the First Step criminal justice reform bill backed by President Trump, we should hail this great accomplishment -- much needed for prison sentencing reform. The Senate version of the bill went to the House, which passed it, and the President signed it.

Essentially the bill will allow thousands of prisoners to obtain an earlier release from prison and reduce many more prison sentences in the future, so it will contribute to reduced incarceration. Among other things, the bill will protect first-time offenders from mandatory minimum sentences and ease the three strikes rule. As a result, prisoners with three or more convictions, including for drug offenses, will get 25 years instead of life. In addition, inmates can earn more good time credits by avoiding a disciplinary record, and they can get earned time credits by participating in more vocational and rehabilitative programs, Then, they can be released early to halfway houses or home confinement when not actually working.

Besides reducing prison overcrowding, the educational programs can provide ex-cons with new job skills, so they are less likely to commit new crimes and therefore the bill also helps to reduce recidivism.

The passage of this bill is critical, because for decades, the sentencing laws have unfairly impacted minority communities and contributed to the high rate of poverty and crime in the inner cities.

As the President has pointed out in support of this bipartisan bill, it will make our communities safer and give ex-cons a second chance at life after they have served their time. Thus, besides making America safer, this bill will reduce the unnecessary costs for imprisoning low-level offenders with long sentences. Accordingly, it makes sense to finally change our sentencing laws to create a "win-win" for prisoners, their families and American society as a whole. At least this is one bill that has wide support from virtually all social and economic groups in America. Now that this bill has passed to change the sentencing for federal prisoners, this will serve as a model for the states to similarly change their sentencing laws.

I have long favored such reforms in writing about on crime and criminal justice, and in writing about the prisons in *The Costly U.S. Prison System, Crime in America,* and the forthcoming *Prisons in America,* I have recommended that sentencing laws be changed in exactly the way described in the bill. Among other things, it provides more rehabilitation efforts for prisoners and enables judges to exercise more discretion in sentencing nonviolent offenders to reduced sentences, especially for drug offenses. The advantage of doing so is that rehabilitated non-violent ex-offenders are less likely to reoffend, resulting in lower levels of recidivism, which means a re-arrest following the prisoner's release. Shorter sentences also help to keep the families of ex-cons together. Additionally, ex-cons who are better able to find jobs and become productive citizens have less need to return to crime.

The passage of this bill is especially critical, because for decades, the sentencing laws have unfairly impacted minority communities and contributed to the high rate of poverty and crime in the inner cities. But now it seems Congress, along with the President, have finally come together in a spirit of bipartisanship to support this bill, which will make America safer. At the same time, besides contributing to a safer America, this bill will reduce the unnecessary costs of imprisoning low-level offenders with long sentences.

In short, this reform bill is long overdue, since it makes sense to change our sentencing laws to create a positive opportunity for prisoners, their families, and American society as a whole. The bill has wide support from virtually all social and economic groups in America. This law to change the sentencing for federal prisoners will serve as a model for the states to similarly change their sentencing laws.

This bill is also especially important because it appeals to both conservatives and liberals. On the one hand, the bill incorporates conservatives' concerns with creating a more efficient cost-effective prison system. And on the other hand, it addresses liberals' concern with helping prisoners become reintegrated into the community, keep their family together, and get the necessary training to get a job. So it's also a "win-win" for both sides of the aisle, in addition for the prisoners, prisoners, their families, and society as a whole.

CHAPTER 10: BIPARTISAN PASSAGE OF PRISON SENTENCE REFORM BILL

Finally! In an unusual display of BIPARTISANSHIP, on December 20, the House passed the Senate prison reform bill called The First Step Act. It sailed through the Senate by a vote of 87 to 12 and the House by a vote of 358 to 36. The bill is one of its last acts before Congress adjourned for the Christmas holidays and a new Congress began its term in January. Finally the bill was signed. They got it done. Bravo to all.

The announcement of the bill's passage was largely lost in the hysteria over the government shutdown, the President's announced pullout of troops from Syria and potentially from Afghanistan, the nose dive of the stock market, and liberal hype about the Mueller probe. But it's important to recognize this historic Congressional achievement which President Trump, a long-time backer of the bill, signed the very next day. The President called it "an incredible success for our country." Then, he went on to say "When both parties work together we can keep our country safer." The President had previously endorsed the bill as offering "reasonable sentencing reforms while keeping dangerous and violent criminals off our streets." It has been called the most far-reaching overhaul of the criminal justice system in a generation.

The bipartisan passage of this bill is a great achievement not only for its goal of reforming sentencing but because it shows that members of Congress can work together for the common good. It's wonderful to see members on both sides of the aisle finally put aside their differences to support a bill that the vast majority of Americans also support.

This widespread support has been reflected in various public opinion polls, such as one by the Benenson Strategy Group in October 2017, in which 70-72% of the respondents indicated it was important to reduce the prison population. The respondents also stated that they were more likely to vote for an elected official who supported eliminating mandatory minimum laws, or who agreed that incarceration is often counterproductive to public safety.

More recently a poll by the John D. and Catherine T. MacArthur Foundation found widespread public support for rehabilitation efforts in local criminal justice systems. For example, as reported by Kathryn Casteel in a February 13, 2018 article on the FiveThirtyEight website, 71% of the respondents said rehabilitation or treatment is the most important consideration in sentencing someone who has been convicted of a nonviolent crime and has a mental illness. Additionally, 84% of respondents said local governments should devote resources to providing substance abuse treatment to drug abusers.

What this bipartisan vote shows is that we may not agree on many things these days in our divisive political environment, but at least the vast majority of us can agree on the need to give prisoners convicted of serious non-violent crimes a second chance at life outside prison. And while this fact isn't often mentioned, by increasing rehabilitation, this bill will reduce recidivism and help to cut down prison costs. That's because these prisoners will be less likely to turn to crime, due to improved job skills.

Additionally, this legislation will help bring together and support families fractured due to a family member being in prison.

This bill offers even more hope for the future because the much needed changes in the federal sentencing law can provide a model for the states, which have many more prisoners. Now state officials can look to this law to follow in reforming their own sentencing practices, and so can officials legislating policies for those held in jails run by local municipalities.

The major advantages of the bill are that it shortens sentences for deserving prisoners and provides for increased rehabilitation efforts. As a result, prisoners are better able to find jobs and live productive lives when they return to their communities. And they are more likely to return to intact families, too. Among other things, the bill provides these major changes:

- Three-strikes prisoners will no longer face automatic life sentences; instead they will only face 25 years.

- Drug offenders who would automatically receive 20 year sentences will now face only 15 years.

- Well-behaved low-risk prisoners will get credit for participating in job-training programs and will have more opportunities to participate in early release programs.

- Corrections officers will get de-escalation training to help them better respond to inmates with mental illnesses or cognitive impairment.

The bill has received extensive support across the political spectrum, including on the left by the American Civil Liberties Union and on the right by the American Conservative Union, the Fraternal Order of the Police, and the Faith and Freedom Coalition. A key reason for this widespread support is that the bill gives non-violent, low-risk offenders a chance for a fresh start as productive members of society, and at the same time, it keeps dangerous and violent prisoners behind bars, making communities safer.

Now since this bill has been signed into law, I hope to see other recommendations I have made for all phases of the criminal justice process turned into legislation. For instance, I have encouraged legislation to enable judges to exercise more discretion in sentencing nonviolent offenders to reduced sentences, especially for drug offenses. As I have repeatedly pointed out in my books, reducing recidivism is key. Shorter sentences help lower levels of recidivism, since they help to keep the families of felons and ex-felons together, resulting in lower levels of recidivism. Then, too, these ex--felons are better able to find jobs and become productive citizens, so they have still less incentive to return to crime.

CHAPTER 11: WHAT'S NEXT AFTER PASSAGE OF BILL ON PRISON SENTENCE REFORM ACT?

Now that the House and Senate passed the Senate reform bill and President Trump signed it before a new Congress begins its term in January, the question is "What's next?" The bipartisan support for the bill means that it will be up to the Congress to pass any needed supplemental legislation to provide any needed additional funding to implement the bill.

The bill is also an excellent model for the state legislatures to pass their own bills to make changes in the state and local prisons, since the vast majority of prisoners are held in such prisons. For example, according to Bureau of Justice Statistics, of the 2.1 million prisoners in the U.S. in 2016, 91% or 1.9 million were in state prisons, a rate of 780 per 100,000 adults. Accordingly, I hope to take a campaign for prison reform to the state governors and legislators next.

This reform should occur, since there is widespread support for this reform throughout the U.S. A major concern has been reducing the size of the prison population, both to save costs and to provide rehabilitation and treatment to prisoners committing less serious non-violent crimes.

This emphasis on cost-cutting and rehabilitation is crucial, because it will also cut down on recidivism, since these prisoners will be less likely to turn to crime due to improved job skills. Plus this approach will help bring together and support families which have been broken up due to a family member being in prison.

These changes in federal sentencing law can provide a model for the states for their prisons and for local municipalities for their jails. In particular, that will mean shorter sentences for deserving inmates and increased rehabilitation that can occur both in prison or jail and in the local community. In turn, prisoners will be better able to find jobs and live productive lives once back in their community. And they will be more likely to return to intact families.

Among other things, the states should adopt these provisions of the federal bill:

At least passing this bill on reforming the prison system, shows that bipartisan support is possible, and can show the way to making these many other needed reforms in the criminal justice system.

PART 4: HEALING THE DIVISIONS IN AMERICAN SOCIETY

CHAPTER 12: HOW DIVISIONS IN US AFFECT CRIME AND WHAT TO DO

The 2018 election has revealed the deep divisions present in American society, and repeatedly liberal news commentators and pundits have pointed this out. They have talked about the women's vote leading to more women getting elected to office, Latino voters being influenced by the immigration conflict, older voters being especially concerned about health care, rural voters being Trump's primary supporters, and so on.

And the statistics show how different racial, ethnic, and age groups commit different kinds of crimes and experience different results at all phases of the criminal justice system -- from rates of arrest to conviction to sentencing to getting released on probation or parole. In general, the poor and minority group members fare much worse. Much could be done to reduce the extra costs in how the system processes these individuals. Also, much could be done to help produce more productive citizens less likely to return to crime. But conservatives and liberals are wide apart on how to resolve these problems.

What can be done about it? In the following section, I'll provide some ideas on what to do, drawing in part on a discussion of these many divisions in *Crime in America* and *Fractured America*. The goal is to help incarcerated individuals become more productive citizens, preserve family unity, and create stronger communities, despite divisions between groups based on race, ethnicity, income, culture, and other factors.

CHAPTER 13: RESEARCH ON IDENTITY POLITICS SHOWS WHY AMERICA IS SO DIVIDED

THE DIVIDED STATES OF AMERICA

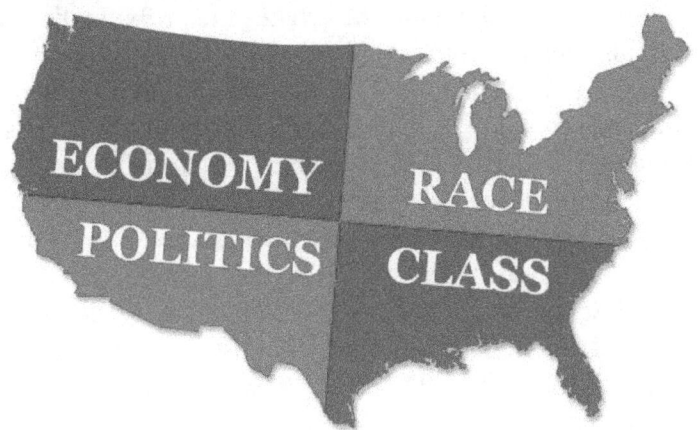

Why is America so divided? A growing body of research now points to the many psychological factors which contribute to this growing divide. This research suggests a solution, too.

Some key findings are the following.

1) The divisions in current U.S. politics are less about the issues than about being part of a team, such as "Team Red" or "Team Blue," as described in a September 2018 *Psychology Today* article "Why Has America Become So Divided" by Joe Pierre, M.D. His explanation is that individuals take sides by turning the other side into "us" versus "them" conflict. As a result, liberals become "libtards" while conservatives become "fascists," so there is no basis for finding common ground. An example of this split played out with disastrous results in the U.S. Government Shutdown, where President Trump and Speaker of the House Nancy Pelosi confronted each other like members of opposing teams in sports, and making the slightest concession in playing the game meant the other side wins.

2) The polarization is also furthered by the news media, which likes controversy because it sells stories. So the messages from increasingly divisive political campaigns are emphasized by the media, which repeats the same messages again and again. As a consequence, increasingly Republicans get their news from Fox News, while Democrats tune into MSNBC, CNN, and the late night comics like Stephen Colbert.

3) The social media exacerbates the problem, because individuals seek out sources for information that support their point of view, while they pay less attention to or actively screen out information sources that contradict their own bias. It's a phenomenon called "confirmation bias" and this bias plays a major role in helping individuals choose and stay with the chosen side.

4) The power of identity politics, rather than issues, also contributes to the partisan divide, such as described by Cameron Brick and Sander van der Linden in a June 2018 *Scientific American Article:* "How Identity, Not issues, Explains the Partisan Divide." Unfortunately, the divide goes far beyond disagreements on policy. As Brick and van der Linden point out, liberals and conservatives in America not only disagree on policy, but they are "increasingly unwilling to live near each other, be friends, or get married to members of the other group. This rejection based on group membership is called *affective polarization*, meaning that our feelings (affect) are different towards members of our own group compared to outsiders."

This great split between individuals on each side is a terrible outcome, because disagreements about policies don't have to lead to growing intolerance. However, that has been happening, as individuals on both sides increasingly distrust each other, leading to growing gridlock in Congress. A prime example is the effort by Democrats in the House to prevent the passage of a funding bill for the Wall and then undermine President Trump's effort to get this funding by declaring a national emergency. Additionally, there is growing physical violence on both sides, including counter-protests to conservative efforts to present their point of view. One such example is the liberals' desire to take down the statues of Confederate military heroes, even though they remain a part of history

And it gets worse and worse, because Americans increasingly don't just disagree about the issues, but they are less and less willing to socialize with others who have different views. So that contributes to building barriers between either side of the divide.

In turn, these divisions have led to increasing tribalism and groups that identify based on race, ethnicity, gender, religion, and other social associations, as described in more detail in *Fractured America.*

CHAPTER 14: HOW THE LEFT HAS CONTRIBUTED TO THE DIVISIONS IN AMERICA

Commonly, liberals and the media blame the right wing supporters of President Trump and represent them as redneck crazies. However, there is evidence that the left has played a major part in creating or exacerbating differences in America, and even the British have noted this divisiveness, such as in a seminal article "How America's Identity Politics Went from Inclusion to Division" by Amy Chua in a March 2018 issue of *The Guardian*.

Following are some key explanations for how identity politics in America changed from urging inclusion to promoting division. Then, I will recommend some fixes.

One major source of divisiveness is the declining proportion of Americans who are white. While minority concerns about discrimination have been highlighted and shamed in the media, any protests by white Americans who are becoming a minority are met with charges of racism and white nationalism. Yet white Americans feel a tremendous loss of power because of what they feel is an influx of immigrants taking unfair advantage of our system. At the same time, the higher birth rate among Latin Americans and blacks has decreased the relative percentage of whites in the population. In fact, in her article, Chua cites a 2012 study which showed that more than half of white Americans believed that whites have become the primary victims of discrimination, rather than blacks.

Under the circumstances, as a threatened group, many white Americans have felt mistreated and disrespected and have embraced what social scientists call "tribalism", so they have "become more insular, more defensive, more punitive, more us-versus-them," to cite Chua. However, liberals and the media don't recognize this growing fear whites have of being eclipsed by other groups. Rather liberals and the media react to any white protests with derision, feeling the protesters' claims are unjustified. At the same time, liberals sympathize with other minority group members, when they feel they are individually and as a group being attacked. And it is true -- there are growing hate crimes and protests against Jews, Muslim, Latinos, gays, transgendered individuals, and others. But while these individuals and groups are embraced as victims by the media and liberals, any whites who come together to call attention to their own grievances are treated as attackers and labeled as "fascists" and "Nazis," which are terms associated with evil. Or they are called "nationalists" and "white supremacists," liberal code words to label white Americans with a conservative viewpoint as evil.

The leftists have also transformed the meaning of Martin Luther King's ideal that all individuals should be "guaranteed the unalienable rights of life, liberty, and the pursuit of happiness", expressed in his famous "I have a dream" speech. Initially King's deal was supposed to represent a call for universal human rights, based on the dignity of each individual providing the basis for a "just international order." So initially, the Left was especially concerned with the way minorities and disadvantaged groups were oppressed and denied rights, and they promoted the ideal of being blind to group differences. The ideal was bringing everyone together, regardless of ethnicity, race or gender.

But after the Soviet Union collapsed, the Left shifted from being concerned with an unjust capitalist system to recognizing group differences and discrimination. Or to cite Chua's article, "the politics of redistribution was replaced by a 'politics of recognition.' Modern identity politics was born."

This shift in the Left's attitude was the turning point which led the way to singling out and demonizing white Americans. This happened through identity politics, whereby the Left sought recognition for the demands of specific groups, such as women, blacks, and lesbians, that were discriminated against due to their difference from the white heterosexual male ideal. The Left's goal was to get respect for each individual as different, rather than to gain respect in spite of one's differences or to gain inclusion as part of universal humankind.

At the same time, the Left did not grant the same kind of recognition or respect to white Americans. Also, the Left claimed that anyone who tried to deny this recognition of the demands of different groups was guilty of group blindness or oppression of others. Unfortunately, this whole process of identity politics has resulted in more and more subdivisions of groups seeking recognition. It's crazy. Facebook, for example, invites users to choose from over 50 gender designations, which include a variety of new terms to choose from, such as intersex and genderqueer.

Moreover, this emphasis on group identity means that individuals cannot even adopt the dress or ideas of other groups. For instance, a white male who opens a restaurant serving Mexican food could be accused of appropriating that culture, rather than showing an appreciation for it. What's wrong about this approach is that the Left throws accusations around and ultimately presents the white American male and secondarily the white American female as the oppressor. Thus, any time whites have grievances, these are considered illegitimate or mocked by the media. Or the liberals and media argue that these difficulties are well-deserved, such as when white farmers in the South protested that they were losing income due to tariff wars. Often the liberals and media made fun of the white conservatives having financial problems, because "they had voted for Trump", so they deserved being victims.

Under the circumstances, a big problem is that the white Americans have legitimately come to see themselves as an endangered, discriminated group. Indeed they are, as a result of attacks by liberals and the media who have shamed and berated them. The strident verbal attacks on them have become a form of bullying. The liberals and the media don't recognize white Americans as victims. Instead, they have demonized them and downplayed their complaints about economic losses and losing their way of life as illegitimate. Moreover, when white Americans complain about illegal immigrants, they are accused of being racists. However, whites do have a real gripe, because they are losing their place, and many have a declining income in America.

That's why the problem is exactly as Chua states in the conclusion of her article. While black Americans, Asian Americans, Hispanic Americans, Jewish Americans, and many others are allowed -- indeed, encouraged -- to feel solidarity and take pride in their racial or ethnic identity, white Americans have for the last several decades (been told) they must never ever do so. And that is not fair.

So what's the solution? A good starting point is to recognize and respect the legitimacy of the complaints of white Americans. Their complaints should be seen as equally valid as the claims of other groups. Then, with that understanding, there is a need to have discussions, perhaps with representatives of the different groups, and to issue a report to the media. As for what else, I hope to suggest some actions that might be taken by the government, the media, and different political groups to bring everyone together again.

PART 5: DEALING WITH ILLEGAL IMMIGRATION

CHAPTER 15: WHAT TO DO ABOUT THE MIGRANTS AT THE BORDER

Recently over 1500 refugees and migrants arrived at the U.S. Mexican border in the city of Tijuana. They claim they are fleeing poverty in their home countries of Honduras, El Salvador, and Guatemala. Meanwhile, about 6000 troops sent by the President Trump are camped on the U.S. side of the border, after building concrete barriers and putting up barbed wire fences to keep them out. So you might say that the two sides are poised for a show-down, or what some might dub a "Mexican stand-off" -- literally.

Now the question is what should we do about the would-be immigrants? Let them in? Keep them out? Or work out some procedure for selecting a small subset of the migrants to let in and send the others back? The debate about what to do is raging furiously, with conservatives generally wanting them to be kept out and liberals wanting to let some or most of them in.

While the mainstream media has generally supported the liberal position, conservatives are right to be wary about the dangers of letting large numbers of immigrants enter the country, especially without sufficient time to vet them.

There is also a danger of letting in younger refugees and asylum seekers, because younger immigrants have a higher rate of crime than other Americans of the same age. Illegals add to the crime rates, if only because their younger age makes them more prone to crime.

Accordingly, I propose several suggestions for fixing the illegal immigration mess, which would apply to deciding how to deal with thousands of refugees and migrants who might arrive in future caravans, many now driven by trucks to speed their journey. Among my suggestions are these:

1) Secure the border with a combination of walls, fences, greater patrols, drones, and more border security agents. This effort can be especially important now in that many individuals may take advantage of their growing numbers to seek alternate pathways into the United States. They might be willing to risk an illegal entry rather than wait for the possibility of a slow entry for a very small number of individuals in the caravan.

2) Discourage illegal immigration by eliminating the access of illegal immigrants to most services provided by city, state, or local governments, which might lead many such immigrants to leave the U.S. voluntarily. Yes, they may be fleeing from some very bad conditions in their home countries. But the U.S. does not have the resources to accommodate a large influx of immigrants. After all, it is now suffering from a variety of homegrown problems, most notably the effects of hurricanes and other storms in the Eastern Seaboard, fires in California, and over 300 mass shootings all over America so far this year.

3) Monitor immigrant crime more closely by requiring the local and state criminal justice departments at all levels -- from the local police to the state attorney general's office and courts -- to keep accurate records of all crimes. They should also include information to indicate whether a person who has been arrested,

tried, convicted, and sentenced to prison is a legal or illegal immigrant and from what country. Then, this data will provide a clearer picture of the extent to which illegal immigrants are involved in criminal activity across the country.

4) Institute strict penalties and deportations for crimes committed by illegal immigrants. Perhaps tag those deported with microchips so they can be more readily identified if they attempt to re-enter the United States.

5) Encourage Hispanic community members to cooperate to support the arrest or deportation of illegal immigrants engaged in criminal activity.

6) Limit the number of legal immigrants allowed into the U.S. each year and be more selective about the immigrants admitted in order to select those who offer the most skills and education, and therefore are better able to contribute to American society. However, we must take care not to have them take away jobs from Americans.

Certainly, one can sympathize with the tragic situation of the migrants and refugees having to flee their country. But this migration is part of a much larger problem of over 65 million displaced persons, including over 25 million refugees worldwide due to wars, poverty, and turmoil within their countries. Unfortunately, these people have few options, and most of them are ending up in refugee camps and tent cities or becoming homeless.

As much as one might sympathize with their plight, it is not possible for other countries to incorporate this many displaced persons into their countries, especially when these refugees speak another language. The danger is destabilizing the host country and creating an even greater risk of crime and disorder in that country. The same is true for the migrants and refugees trying to get into America. It is simply not possible to take in the vast majority of them without creating even more crime and dissension within the U.S.

CHAPTER 16: GLOBAL IMMIGRATION CRISIS REQUIRES RESTRICTIONS

The global immigration crisis is very real and has the potential to destabilize countries around the world. Liberals try to paint any country leaders trying to protect their country as insensitive and even evil. This effort by liberals has led to a growing barrage of attacks on the Trump administration for its policies to crack down on immigration on our Southern border. As part of these attacks, there have been photos and stories of the suffering faced by immigrants who have been caught trying to sneak into the United States. There have been stories about children separated from their parents and the terrible conditions for the immigrants coming from Mexico and all of Central America. And the President's proposal to build a wall has met with outright derision, as if it was the only strategy, rather than one of many methods to stem the immigration tide.

However, the huge influx of immigrants seeking entry to wealthier countries is a serious risk. Accordingly, it is important not to let the sympathetic portraits of individual immigrants who have suffered in their home country and in their journey to America undermine the serious danger to the U.S. if immigration policies are not tightened.

An important consideration is that the battle over immigration to America is part of a global crisis in which there are more migrants than ever. This huge influx requires new regulations to deal with the hordes that could upend the economy, as well as to keep out the criminals, including drug dealers, who are seeking refuge in America. A big problem is that the old laws protecting immigrants have become obsolete in light of the crisis.

Back in 1951, the United Nations established some definitions and regulations for refugees and asylum seekers, giving them broad protections wherever they happened to flee to. For example, as described by a September 2018 article in *The Guardian,* "Migration: How Many People Are on the Move around the World" by Amelia Hill, an asylum seeker is someone who has left their country and is seeking protection from persecution. A refugee is someone who has already received such protection after fleeing from terrible conditions in their home country. In either case, the UN policy is that all refugees and asylum seekers should have the right to international protection, meaning that anyone should be allowed to enter another country to seek asylum.

By contrast, a migrant, such as someone who is just seeking a better job and better life, shouldn't be granted such protections. However, the distinctions have become less clear now, since many immigrants are leaving their home country because they are suffering from poverty, a limited food supply, and economic and social turmoil. But whether those conditions might qualify them to be considered asylum seekers or refugees, the distinctions shouldn't matter, because the vast hordes of immigrants, whatever their status, are threatening the stability of their destination countries. That's because the numbers of migrants have become so vast that these destination countries can't accommodate them without losing their essential character and economic strength.

Thus, in spite of the images of suffering mothers, emaciated children, and jailed husbands, the danger to the entire country has to be considered, given the huge number of migrants -- much larger than the world has ever seen.

As pointed out in an article in *The Guardian* and on the Doctors Without Borders website, there are now 68.5 million forcibly displaced people around the world, which is a much greater number than at any time in human history. Certainly, these migrants have a compelling reason to leave their home countries because of the dangers they faced there, such as continued bombing, an invading army, gang violence, and threats of being extorted or killed by terrorists. They have sought refuge in more stable countries, such as the U.S., Canada, and Germany, in order to gain protection from violence and access to food, shelter, and medical care. Under international law they are supposed to have this right.

However, this expectation has come up against real limits on the ground because of the threat from the vast number of immigrants now seeking shelter. That is why increasingly governments from more stable countries around the world have been closing their borders and enacting policies to keep migrants from seeking asylum, policies that liberals point to as inhumane.

But why shouldn't the U.S., like other governments, protect its borders? This border security is critical, or we could lose the essence of what we are as a country, which is why such a large percentage of the population supports tightening up border restrictions.

So what countries are most threatened? And by whom? There's an interesting article in *The Guardian* article that describes the key destination countries and where most of the refugees and asylum seekers are coming from. According to 2015 statistics in this article, the U.S., along with Germany, Russia, Saudi Arabia, and the U.K., traditionally have been the five main destination countries, while Mexico, along with India, Russia, China, and Bangladesh, have been the top five origin countries. However, the recent crises in Syria and Myannmar may have made them among the top origination countries.

A big problem for the U.S. in this equation of who's going to and coming from where, is that it has historically accepted more refugees than any other country in the world, though this number has slowed in recent years, as *The Guardian* article states. But that number has been changing, and it has to. For example, in 2016, the U.S. took in 85,000 refugees, and this number was reduced to 45,000 in 2017 under President Trump, with only about 21,000 expected in in 2018. Liberals feel the U.S. should be much more open, but there are serious consequences for having much more open borders.

A good example is what happened in Europe and especially Germany. Europe was swamped with millions of refugees coming from the Middle East and Africa, due to wars in Syria, Afghanistan, ISIS activities in Iraq, and conflicts throughout Africa, as described in a February *Time* article, "Dividing Lines: The Human Face of Global Migration." As a result of this massive migration, voters in Europe have viewed this migration as "out of control." Anti-immigration politicians throughout Europe, campaigning on the promise of limiting migration and protecting Europe's Judeo-Christian culture, gained power. Likewise, President Trump's anti-immigration policies are widely promoted throughout the West. This has resulted in victories for anti-immigration politicians in Sweden, Slovenia, Hungary, Italy, and Czechoslovakia, and fueling the anger in Britain that led to Brexit, in part to take back the country from the threatening hordes.

What happened in Germany is an example of the danger of opening up the country to immigrants. With the encouragement of German chancellor Angela Merkel, Germany let in about a million immigrants, resulting in Merkel ultimately being forced out of power after 13 years in power, according to a January 29, 2019 *Bloomberg* article: "How Merkel Lost Her Grip." Thus, it's no wonder that in France, the French parliament passed a new law that speeds up deportations of those seeking jobs in Europe, and French

President Emmanuel Macron had this to say: "We cannot take on the misery of the world," as noted in the *Time* article.

So that's what we need to do here. As tough as it may seem to individual immigrants, for the sake of the country we have to crack down on immigration at our borders. Liberals may argue that immigrants will contribute to the economy, and the liberals may show desperate immigrants who are suffering in their trek to get to and across the border. But the massive migration in Mexico and Central America is part of this larger global migration problem, and we simply cannot absorb more immigrants without threatening the stability and character of America.

CHAPTER 17: WHY A WALL ON THE BORDER MAKES SENSE

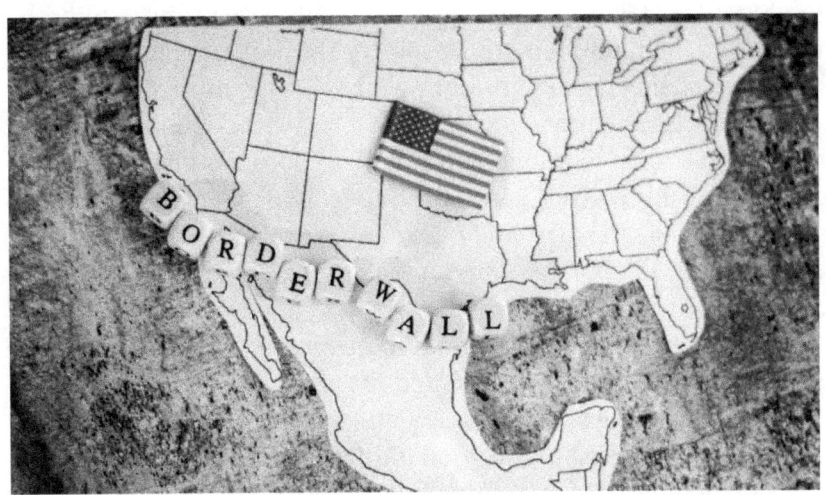

Again and again the liberal media, politicians, and activists have derided the Wall on the border as being a fantasy solution to the problem of illegal immigration. They have claimed the Wall will have little effect in keeping anyone out, because most immigrants come through regular ports of entry, even by air. Or they come by sea or tunnel under walls.

However, there is new evidence and thinking that shows why the Wall will help to stem the flood of illegal immigrants.

For example, in a June 2017 article on the Prager University website, "Build the Wall," the late great conservative columnist Charles Krauthammer observed that, every sensible immigration policy has two goals. One is to "regain control of our borders so that *we* decide who enters." The second is to "find a humane way to deal with the 11 million illegal immigrants who now live among us."

These are reasonable goals that both liberals and conservatives can agree on. So the issue is more about what works to achieve these goals. While liberals decry the ideal of building a wall, it actually works as one of a number of strategies to reduce illegal immigration.

Along with Krauthammer, I believe it is not practical or moral to expel 11 million immigrants. But there is a way to both incorporate them into American society short of legalization and reduce future illegal immigration, which is what most Americans who oppose legalization actually fear. And that's where the wall and other methods to regain control of the border come in. Of course, the wall by itself is not the only way, since we also need cameras, sensors, drones, and beefed up border patrols. But walls help to reduce the number of people who seek to get across the border.

In a July 2017 article in the *Washington Times*, "Beyond the Good News of the Wall," Brandon Judd makes the point that a secure border requires multiple levels of protection, including the Wall. As he points out, a secured border fence, such as the double-layered fencing called for in the bipartisan Secure Fence Act of 2006, which authorized and partially funded the construction of 700 miles of physical fence/barriers along the Mexican border. President Trump has pledged to build an even longer and more secure wall, would be another level of deterrence to those seeking to enter illegally. Having the wall helps to convince people not to break the law in the first place. As a result, it reduces the number of people trying to come to the U.S. to get jobs or public benefits, since they feel they are less likely to succeed. With fewer immigrants trying to enter, the Border Patrol can focus more on keeping the people who are more dangerous and violent from getting into the country.

For example, dangerous criminal cartels can be discouraged from human and drug trafficking, such as that headed up by Joaquin "El Chapo" Guzman, who was recently convicted in Brooklyn for leading one of the biggest cartels in Mexico. Yes, the drug traffickers use cars, trucks, boats, tunnels, and other means to get their drugs into America. New technologies for better screening at entry points will help to keep out much of this traffic. If a strong wall or border fence can discourage the vast number of economic migrants from coming in, this enables the Border Patrol and Customs agents to respond to and arrest the people who are truly dangerous. In other words, I agree with Judd that the huge number of migrants viewing the U.S. as a land of economic opportunity provides cover for the small number of dangerous migrants.

Another good reason to build the wall is to discourage the coyotes and traffickers in human slavery who are exploiting the illegal immigrants by taking advantage of their desperation in trying to cross the border. At the same time, we can increase the number of families and other immigrants admitted legally. That's a recommendation proposed by James D. Miller in a Fox News article, "To Solve the Immigration Crisis, Build the Border Wall and Admit More Legal Immigrants."

Still another reason to build a wall is because they help to control a border. For example, all over Europe, countries are building fences on the border to keep out the millions of Middle Eastern refugees. Among the countries building them are Hungary, Bulgaria, Austria, Greece, Spain, and Norway. And of course Israel has put up a wall on the West Bank. Furthermore, to cite Krauthammer's report, building a triple fence outside of San Diego resulted in reducing migrants crossing the border there by 90 percent.

In short, there are many reasons that walls do work. Moreover, they stand as a symbol of the country's resolve to secure its borders. The border alone won't be the sole solution, and there will be ways to breach it. But the wall doesn't have to be completely secure. It mainly has to reduce the huge influx of migrants to a more manageable level, which makes it possible to take other steps, such as creating a more foolproof electronic verify system that makes it very difficult for illegal immigrants to work in the U.S. Also, the U.S. should have a better visa tracking system, since a very large percentage of illegal immigrants -- about 40% of them according to Krauthammer -- simply overstay their visas.

Thus, in contrast to the liberals' dire warnings that building the Wall is a folly, it makes good sense to build it, along with taking other measures to regain control of our country by reducing the illegal immigration mess.

PART 6: DEALING WITH THE OPIOID CRISIS

CHAPTER 18: WHAT TO DO ABOUT THE OPIOID ABUSE CRISIS

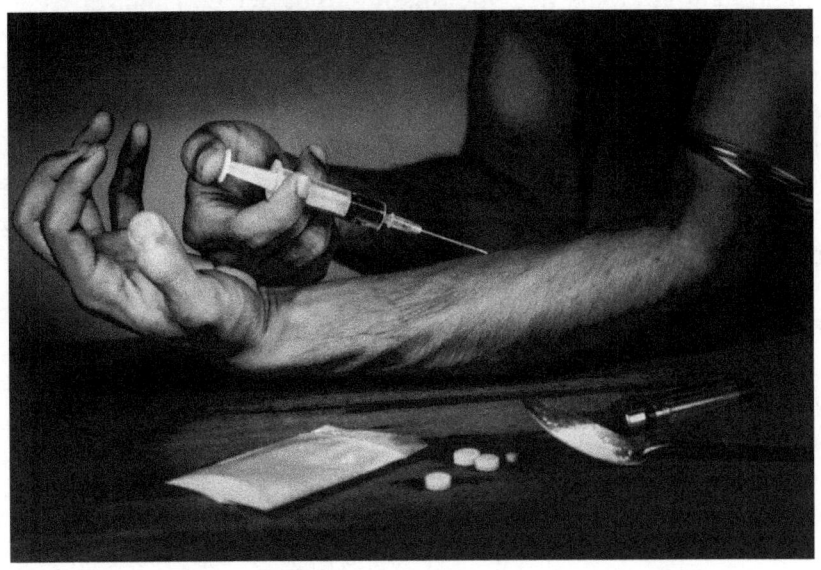

Everyone agrees there is an opioid crisis in America. There were more than 72,000 drug overdose deaths in 2017 from both illicit drugs and prescription opioids, as I noted in *Crime in America.* This number reflects an upward climb each year since 2002, according to the Center for Disease Control's CDC Wonder database. Another troubling statistic is that more than 115 people in the U.S. die each day after overdosing on opioids. And the economic burden on prescription opioid misuse is $78.5 billion a year, which includes the costs of healthcare, lost productivity, addiction treatment, and criminal justice involvement.

Yet given the need to resolve this crisis, the U.S. Congress has so far failed to come up with a bipartisan response in adopting the Opioid Crisis Response Act of 2018. The bill received a 99-1 vote in the Senate on September 17, after the House passed its own bill in June, though the two still have to be reconciled before they can be passed. Unfortunately, this reconciliation seems difficult to achieve, since experts and activists claim the bill doesn't go far enough, mainly because it doesn't significantly increase the spending for the crisis, apart from authorizing some relatively small grant programs with the funding to be decided later in Congress. Also, the bill doesn't pay for a wide expansion of addiction treatment, which many experts believe is necessary.

And now it would seem that the bill has died in Congress, since after a spate of articles in September hailed this bipartisan compromise, nothing further has been done to finalize the bill. Perhaps this is because all interest turned to the elections, and now it's up to a new Congress to deal with the issue.

Thus, we need to let legislators and the media know about the need to act quickly to stem this growing epidemic. We especially need to crack down on the dealers who are furthering addiction while lining their pockets, despite the widely known dangers of drug overdoses. That's why I'm in favor of several policies that have been recommended by the President. These include the following:

- Establish mandatory minimum sentencing as a penalty for distributing certain opioids, based on the amount of drugs seized to help reduce the supply.

- Increase the interdiction efforts at all ports of entry and along U.S. borders.

- Expand access to proven treatments and recovery methods.

- Broaden education and awareness of the crisis.

In addition, I have recommended these additional approaches in my book *Crime in America*:

- Set up a separate division in the prisons or separate prison wings to house drug traffickers.

- Publicize the names of the individuals sentenced under the new laws.

- Set up a tip line for information that leads to the arrest of drug traffickers.

- Provide more funds for research into better addiction treatments.

Based on these recommendations, my goal is to get legislators to incorporate these ideas into the next iteration of the Opioid Crisis Response Act to help reduce the use and abuse of opioids in America.

CHAPTER 19: THE ADVANTAGES OF THE OPIOID CRISIS ACT OF 2018 AND A FEW RESERVATIONS

In all of the turmoil over investigations about Russian influence in U.S. elections and the attention paid to the bipartisan First Step Sentence Reform Act, another act passed by Congress has gone relatively unnoticed. However, Congress' recent passage of the Opioid Crisis Response Act of 2018 (OCRA) in October is an important step in combating the growing opioid use disorder.

At least the provisions of this current bill are a good start. They include the following provisions:

- Reauthorizing $500 million in funding each year to combat opioid use disorder.

- Proving for further access to treatment and recovery services for addicts.

- Giving the National Institutes of Health the authority to more quickly authorize research on alternative pain therapies instead of opioids.

Such provisions are sorely needed because of the huge number of deaths from the opioid epidemic. According to the

National Vital Statistics System Mortality File, over 700,000 people died from drug overdoses between 1999 and 2017, and about 68% of over 70,200 drug overdose deaths in 2017 were due to an opioid. These numbers work out to an average of 130 Americans dying every day from an opioid overdose. And that's clearly unacceptable.

Another benefit of the act is that it will help to reduce homelessness, another growing crisis in cities around America. To this end, the bill recognizes the importance of stable housing as a critical part of treatment and recovery, such as noted in an October article on the EndHomelessness.org website, "The Opioid Crisis Response Act of 2018: What Does It Mean for People Experiencing Homelessness" by Chandra Crawford. This help in reducing homelessness through assistance with overcoming addiction is particularly important. That's why the Act encourages the states to pay for housing-related services for homeless people with an opioid use disorder (OUD) using Medicaid.

This Act can also help to ameliorate the housing and homeless crisis, although any assistance to resolve this should go beyond just helping addicts.

In other words, OCRA by itself isn't enough to be the complete solution to the opioid epidemic, since government aid shouldn't give preference to homeless drug users over the rest of the homeless. But it has some important key provisions along with funding that can help, and in the future, funding should be expanded to help all of the homeless with housing. At least, this legislation can pave the way to help end the housing crisis in many cities, since all of the homeless should be taken off the streets, so they no longer are an eyesore and embarrassment there. Moreover, they shouldn't just get free housing. Rather, the recipients of aid should have to work for it, too.

Therefore, an additional act should provide services to help all homeless people get off the streets. And part of the act should include a "work for services" provision, so this doesn't become a free ride for the homeless. Additionally, if housing aid is given to addicts, it should be terminated after a year if they continue to use or haven't found a job, since it's not fair to give homeless addicts preferential housing assistance not available to the rest of the homeless.

While this Act may seem like a policy to delight liberals, conservatives will find much to like in this approach, because homelessness negatively impacts local businesses and a city's economy as a whole. For example, people who are homeless and have a drug problem contribute to the general deterioration of the neighborhood by shooting up and leaving needles on the street. Or they end up in jail or prison for selling drugs to support their habit. So helping the homeless through this act is not only a more humane approach to dealing with the opioid crisis, but it makes perfect economic sense to do so, resulting in a cleaner city, a stronger retail community, and more sales to tourists.

In short, the Act is designed to achieve the goals of getting the homeless with a drug problem off the streets and into housing in various ways, as described in Crawford's article on "The Opioid Crisis Response Act of 2018." For example, the Secretary of Health and Human Services (HHS) is supposed to issue a report to Congress in a year highlighting the new programs from the states that have led to better treatment outcomes or increased housing stability through providing Medicaid for the homeless with OUD. Additionally HHS plans to provide technical assistance to help the states develop or expand their housing supports to most homeless people.

Still another benefit of the act is that it authorizes community block grants through 2023 to provide funds for temporary housing for up to two years for a group of homeless people with OUD who are in treatment. The pilot program is designed to help states with the highest rates of drug overdose deaths combined with other factors, such as having a high rate of unemployment. Thus, this act both helps the homeless with a drug problem and the local economy where joblessness is high. In fact, there is a close connection between these two problems, in that helping the homeless overcome their drug problem and find housing can help them find jobs.

CHAPTER 20: HOW DRUG COMPANIES HAVE FUELED THE OPIOID CRISIS

Commonly, the widely-recognized opioid crisis is blamed on drug dealers, including illegal immigrants who are bringing in drugs across the border. But among the biggest villains are the manufacturers of these drugs. They have greatly contributed to the crisis with their marketing to both doctors and the general public, as I learned in researching the opioid crisis for a chapter in *Crime in America* and in *Dealing with Illegal Immigration and the Opioid Crisis.*

While illegal immigration is one factor, an even more serious one is the high-powered sales and marketing techniques of drug manufacturers. They are generally able to engage in these promotional activities legally, and the public is largely unaware of their role in contributing to the crisis.

How did this happen and what can we do about it? Here are some explanations and suggestions on what to do.

A first consideration is that both prescription and illegal opioids are often abused because they are so addictive. They are so addictive, because, as reported by the National Institute of Drug Abuse in an article on "The Neurobiology of Drug Addiction," opioid medications bind to opiate receptors in the brain reward areas, so the person not only feels less or no pain, but pleasure. Then, as his or her brain gets used to these feelings and likes them, an opioid user develops increasing tolerance to the dug and has to take more and more of the drug to produce the same level of pain relief and well-being. As a result, the individual becomes dependent and later becomes addicted. Even Rush Limbaugh became addicted to opioid pills and had to struggle to overcome this problem.

That reduction of pain and the increase of pleasure is the basic driver leading individuals to want more and more of the drug. At the same time, the drug companies actively promote the use of these drugs to doctors, pharmacists, and individual users to increase demand. The doctor and pharmacist respond to that demand. Then, individuals eagerly want more, get hooked, and may resort to illicit opioids, which can lead to an overdose in many cases.

Some recent statistics from experts and government agencies show the extent of this crisis. According to experts, over 2 million Americans have become dependent on or have abused prescription or street drugs for both pain relief and pleasure. In 2017, there were over 72,000 overdose deaths, including 49,068 that involved opioid drugs, according to the Center for Disease Control. Over 130 people died each day from drug overdoses in 2016 and 2017, based on data from the U.S. Department of Health and Human Services (HHS).

Some other statistics about addiction are that 11.4 million Americans misused prescription pain medicines in 2016 and in 2017 according to HHS. Another finding is that many people who become dependent on pain pills may start taking heroin instead, because it is less expensive than prescription drugs. According to National Institute of Drug Abuse estimates, about half of younger heroin abusers first abused prescription painkillers, and three out of four new heroin users got their start using prescription drugs.

These statistics are horrendous and the opioid epidemic is only getting worse. It's not just illegal drugs, but overprescribing by doctors and other health professionals. A major reason for this overprescribing is the promotional efforts of the drug companies.

This epidemic started with the overprescribing of legal pain medications, beginning in the 1990s, with opioid medications, such as oxycodone, hydrocodone, and morphine, to treat pain. At first these medications were popular for treating patients after they had surgery or if they were being treated for cancer. But in the last 15 years, doctors have increasingly prescribed these pills for chronic conditions, such as pains in the back, joints, or muscles. More recently, people have turned increasingly to synthetic opioids, such as fentanyl, which is much stronger than heroin -- 50 times as strong -- as well as cheaper, so more and more people have used it. Unfortunately, it can easily be lethal, especially when combined with alcohol, cocaine, or other drugs. It's like a lethal cocktail, in which the addition of fentanyl caused about 46% of the opioid deaths in 2016. And now it is the most commonly used drug involved in drug overdoses.

This increased death toll from drugs has been fueled by overprescribing by physicians who felt concerned that pain was undertreated. At the same time, the pharmaceutical companies began marketing these drugs even more aggressively, while claiming these drugs had little risk, as described in an article on "The U.S. Opioid Epidemic" by Claire Felter for the Council on Foreign Relations (CFR), updated on January 17, 2019.

Thus, as this CFR article indicates, these drug companies bear much of the blame. They have such high pressure sales tactics that even health-care providers have reported feeling pressure to prescribe opioid medications instead of alternatives, which might include physical therapy or acupuncture. But the prescribers accede to the wishes of the patients requesting these drugs, often because the patients have been influenced by the drug company ads, even if these drugs cost more or are less convenient than just popping a pill.

CHAPTER 21: STUDY SHOWS THAT DRUG COMPANY MARKETING HAS LED TO MORE OVERDOSE DEATHS

One of the biggest villains in the increase in opioid addiction and overdose deaths is the aggressive marketing of the drug companies. And now a growing body of research shows this connection of drug company marketing, opioid addiction, and death from an opioid overdose.

A recent study demonstrates this connection by showing how drug company marketing has led to more overdose deaths. The study was cited in a *Vox* article, published January 25, 2019 by German Lopez: "We Now Have More Proof that Drug Companies Helped Cause the Opioid Epidemic." In recent years, the drug companies have spent billions of dollars each year to promote their drugs to doctors using all kinds of incentives, such as speaking fees, free dinners, and paid trips.

One of the first opioid pills in the 1990s was OxyContin, and the manufacturer, Purdue Pharma, sought to convince the Food and Drug Administration (FDA) and doctors, in spite of evidence to the contrary, that the drug was safe and effective. In this way, the opioid manufacturers convinced doctors to prescribe their drugs more and more.

The result of the efforts of all these drug companies has been more overdose deaths, according to a study reported in the Journal of the American Medical Association (JAMA) Network, where the researchers found more deaths when there was more marketing. The results of the study made it very clear that the marketing led to more opioid prescriptions, which led to more misuse, addiction, and overdoses. In making these drug sales, what seemed to have the most influence was the marketer-to-doctor contact.

Thus, the results clearly show how the drug companies are contributing to the opioid crisis. Certainly other factors have contributed, such as the use of illegal opioids, especially illicit fentanyl, which accounted for 40% of the more than 72,000 opioid overdose deaths in 2017, according to the CDC. The other biggest contributors include heroin and cocaine, accounting for another 40%. This increase in opioid prescriptions due to drug promotions has played a major part, although people are generally unaware of this influence.

So who are the major victims of these overdoses? About 80% are white Americans, especially those without a college degree, in part due to low wages or a lack of jobs. As a result, they turn to drugs as a means of escape, and sometimes that escape leads to death. Then, too, U.S. military veterans are twice as likely as others in the general population to suffer, because many vets suffer chronic pain due to injuries incurred during their service, according to a National Institute of Health study, reported by Claire Felter in her article, "The U.S. Opioid Epidemic," for the Council on Foreign Relations (CFR).

What is to be done? I suggest five critical steps.

1) A first step is creating the awareness of what is causing the problem.

2) A second step is reducing the demand for the drugs by developing new non-addictive pain relievers.

3) A third step is making doctors and health providers aware of how their overprescribing contributes to the problem.

4) A fourth step is more closely monitoring the doctors' prescriptions and enabling them to resist the marketing efforts of the drug manufacturers.

5) Providing medically assisted treatment to addicts before they overdose.

CHAPTER 22: OTHER EVIDENCE THAT DRUG COMPANIES HAVE FUELED THE OPIOID CRISIS

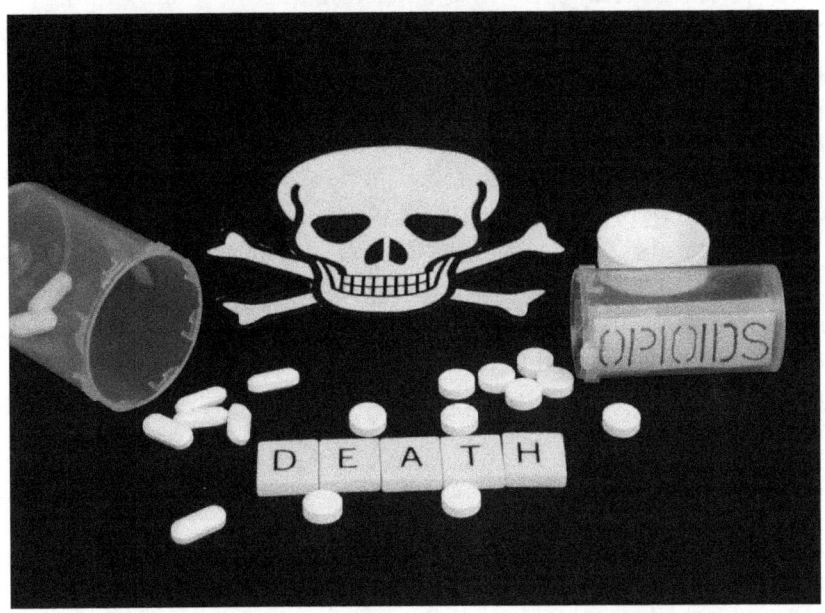

There is growing evidence that the drug companies have helped to cause the opioid overdose crisis due to their aggressive marketing. Besides the previously cited study in JAMA Internal Medicine, even more evidence points the finger squarely at the drug companies.

For example, according to a study reported in a *Vox* article, "We Now Have More Proof that Drug Companies Helped Cause the Opioid Epidemic" by German Lopez, the drug companies played a major role in the first wave of the opioid epidemic which washed into America in three main waves. In the first wave which started in the late 1990s through the early 2000s, doctors prescribed a growing number of opioids to reduce or stop pain. The result was that the drugs spread widely, and often they were misused or led to addiction -- not just among patients, but among their friends and family members. Additionally, teens took drugs they found in their parents' medicine cabinets. Furthermore, many individuals who later became addicts or overdosed got their pills on the black market.

The marketers played a major role in contributing to the epidemic, because they aggressively promoted the drugs to doctors, who then overprescribed drugs to their patients. After that, not only did many patients become addicted, but others could easily access these drugs. The incentive for the drug companies was that they made more and more money, the more drugs they sold, regardless of how those drugs were used.

Then, this first wave opened up the door to the second and third waves. This second wave of overdoses occurred in the 2000s as a result of a growing supply of heroin in the market, as drug dealers and traffickers found a new source of profit in the growing population who used opioids. These users were unable to get more pills from their doctor, or they saw heroin as a cheaper way to reduce the pain.

Then, most recently, the third wave has occurred because of fentanyl, which is an even more powerful and cheaper drug than heroin. But it is much deadlier because of its greater potency, and sometimes dealers mixed it with heroin, because it was cheaper. However, that also meant that users got a more powerful fix that often led to an overdose.

Unfortunately, the drug companies have added to the problem through their aggressive marketing, despite evidence that the drugs weren't a safe or effective alternative to other painkillers on the market. And now a recent lawsuit against the maker of OxyContin shows how the drug companies have used this aggressive marketing to sell their drugs.

As the *Vox* article notes, Massachusetts Attorney General Maura Healey filed a lawsuit against Purdue Pharma, which makes OxyContin. Among other things the suit complained that the company ignored excessive prescribing in the United States, although its staff was warned that the company should have reported the "pill mills" to the federal officials.

Still other reports, such as one by a group of public health experts in the *Annual Review of Public Health,* have pointed to the very irresponsible behavior of the opioid manufacturers. According to this report, the companies exaggerated the safety and benefits of their products. They also supported advocacy groups and education campaigns that promoted the use of opioids. Additionally, they lobbied lawmakers to loosen restrictions on being able to obtain the drugs. They convinced the FDA to approve opioids for chronic use, guaranteeing a huge increase in addition. Not only Purdue was involved in this effort, but so were Endo, Teva, Abbott Laboratories, and other companies making these drugs. Dollars for company officers and shareholders took precedence over public safety.

Unfortunately, the result was that addiction and overdoses increased as did opioid sales. There's even a chart from the *Annual Review of Public Health* that shows this direct connection. As opioid sales rose from 1999 to 2010, so did opioid deaths. What makes this connection even worse is that the drugs are not only deadly, but they aren't as effective against pain as Purdue and the other drug makers claim.

Why not? Because, as the *Vox* article points out, there is only very weak scientific evidence that opioid painkillers can effectively treat long-term chronic pain as patients grow tolerant of opioids' effects. But at the same time, much evidence shows that prolonged use can lead to very bad complications, which include a higher risk of becoming addicted, overdosing, or even dying. In short, the risks and downsides of taking opioids are much greater than any benefits for most patients suffering from pain -- or taking opioids for any other reason.

At least, there has been the beginning of a crackdown on this aggressive marketing by drug companies. For example, in 2007, Purdue Pharma and three top executives were hit with over $630 million in federal fines for misleading the public with their advertising. In addition, the three executives received criminal convictions, though they only received three years of probation and 400 hours of community service. And that seems like a slap on the wrist, when you consider the many lives lost due to their marketing.

Still public sentiment is growing against the drug companies, leading Purdue to announce that it will stop marketing opioids to doctors. And now there may be even more of a crackdown. For example, one Cleveland judge combined several lawsuits against opioid companies in order to seek a big settlement agreement. This would not only result in a financial settlement to pay for treatment for addicts throughout the U.S., but it would also restrict marketing by these companies. And on January 31, 2019, still another suit against Purdue Pharma was filed by the Massachusetts' attorney general's office, accusing it of deceptively marketing its painkillers, including OxyContin.
Among other things, the suit claimed that the company secretly pursued a plan called "Project Tango" to sell both opioids and drugs to treat opioid addiction, while the wealthy owners on the board obtained more than $4 billion in opioid profits.

Thus, this crackdown against the drug companies is more needed than ever, since restricting marketing could help ameliorate the current opioid crisis and avoid a repeat of this crisis in the future.

PART 7: THE ROLE OF POPULAR CULTURE IN THE CRIMINAL JUSTICE CRISIS

CHAPTER 23: CHOICE OF "JUSTICE" CHOSEN AS WORD OF THE YEAR BY MERRIAM-WEBSTER

Given the growing interest in criminal justice issues -- from concerns about killings by police officers to the use of illegal drugs and the fear of illegal immigrants, it's not surprising that Merriam-Webster, the dictionary publishers, chose "justice" as its 2018 word of the year. It's a very good choice indeed!

Merriam-Webster made this choice because the word "justice" has been featured in the daily news cycles for the past months. According to Peter Sokolowski's, the company's editor-at-large, the word "justice" consistently rose to the top 20 to 30 lookups on the company's website. So it showed both a high volume of traffic and a significant increase in lookups during the year.

Ironically, I chose *"Crime in America"* to be the title of my recently published book on conservatives' approaches to criminals, police, criminal justice, and the opioid crisis, since a search on Amazon's database of popular keywords showed "criminal justice" had relatively few hits, compared to "crime" which had much more. "Criminal justice is too abstract and sounds too academic," a book publicity guru told me.

However, now that "justice" has been recognized as a popular word in searches like "racial justice," "obstruction of justice," "social justice," and the "Justice Department," I'm delighted that the word has been properly recognized.

CHAPTER 24: WHEN TV SERIES GLORIFY CRIMINALS AND WHAT TO DO ABOUT IT

Unfortunately, there have been a spate of recent TV series which glorify criminals and relegate cops, prison officials, and other law enforcement professionals to either background characters, or worse, corrupt and otherwise unsympathetic characters. By contrast, the criminals are the protagonists in these dramas, and viewers are supposed to feel sympathetic and empathetic towards them. And in many cases, they are supposed to feel hostile towards the corrupt or inept officials at all levels of the criminal justice system -- especially cops and prison wardens and guards.

One example of this trend is *Making a Murderer,* now in its 2nd season, which makes it appear that the police, prosecutors, and courts in Manitowoc County, Wisconsin, all ganged up against Steven Avery. They allegedly planted evidence and extracted a false confession from a neighbor, Brandon Dassey, who implicated Avery in a rape torture murder. But Avery's new lawyer in the series suggests that there were two other killers and that the local police and officials ganged up against Avery and Dassey, since Avery filed a $36 million suit against the county after he was falsely imprisoned for 18 years for a rape which someone else committed. Another example of this trend to glorify criminals and disparage law enforcement is *Orange Is the New Black,* now in its 7th season, where the prison management and guards are shown variously as inept, money hungry, and brutal in unfairly treating prisoners, especially after the prisoners have rioted because of their poor treatment.

However, such TV series present a very biased portrait of crime and criminal justice. For example, consider the misleading portrait of the police who have been involved in shooting suspected criminals. Often they are demonized by the media, who portray them as eager killers when facing an African-American or Hispanic suspect, rather than a law enforcement officer having to make a split-second decision whether to shoot in self-defense in a potentially deadly encounter. The problem is that too much media attention is given to sympathetic stories about those protesting against police brutality or against the court verdicts exonerating police officers who have correctly employed the use of force guidelines, such as shooting when in fear for their lives. The media and protesters tend to downplay the fact that the suspect had a knife or gun and appeared to be reaching for or about to shoot it. Or they don't point out how the suspect was trying to drive a car at an officer who then shot him.

While I don't specifically write about these films or TV series in my books, my ideas can readily be applied to assessing the misleading perspective in these films or series that present cops, prison officials, and other law enforcement professionals in a bad light. Accordingly, viewers should understand that these films reflect a liberal perspective, and they should be ready to consider the incidents in the film or TV show from a more conservative perspective. For example, they might recognize that the portrait in a TV documentary like *Making a Murderer* is one-sided.

Then, too, viewers might recognize that most prison officials and guards are dealing with a very difficult and dangerous population, and for the most part, they are trying to do the best they can with limited funds. In short, it is necessary to apply a more conservative perspective on how to cut down crime and deal with problems in the criminal justice system in order to counter the usually liberal perspective of most commentators and writers.

Thus, while these TV series often glorify action and violence as a way to hook an audience, we need more everyday community-based solutions to help individuals become more productive citizens, preserve family unity, and create stronger communities. This way, with closer, more cohesive communities, supportive friends, and jobs, individuals have less incentive to return to any type of crime. This strategy works to help ex-cons avoid returning to prison. It might even help to identify prospective mass murderers and keep them from killing anyone. This approach may not be as exciting as a TV show featuring violence and double dealing by the main and supporting characters, but it has been shown to work in many countries and in communities within the U.S.

CHAPTER 25: A WARNING ABOUT THE DANGERS OF COMEDIANS TODAY

Today, the late night comedians have become more popular than ever. For example, according to the TV by the Numbers report for January 19, 2019, Stephen Colbert has 41% of the TV-viewing audience in its time slot, the Late Night with Seth Myers has a 27% viewership, and the Daily Show with Trevor Noah has 23% of the viewers. That turns into about 4 million viewers for Colbert, about 2 ½ million viewers for Myers and 2 million for Noah. Then, over the weekend, Saturday Night Live scores even more viewers -- over 10 million in its 2018 season -- and it spends much of the night skewering President Trump and his administration, with a particularly disrespectful parody of the President by Alec Baldwin.

A key reason for the success of these comedians is their comedy is focused on mocking President Trump, his family, and the Republican Party. In effect, they have become a mouthpiece for the political views of liberals under the cover of comedy, and as such they often present an exaggerated or incorrect view of what is happening today. Then, if they are criticized for their commentary, they can say they were only making jokes. But their jokes can be a political platform, rather than being a humorous commentary of everyday life in general.

At one time, the commentary of comedians used to be about the events of the days or their foibles in everyday life. But today their monologues and many of their guests have turned into a one-sided blast at President Trump and his family. Virtually anything is fair game. The comedians have played up the Russia investigation to make President Trump and his associates seem guilty; they have made fun of his choices to be on the Supreme Court; they have mocked his relationships with foreign powers; they have suggested he is criminally culpable because of his dealings to build a Trump Tower in Moscow; and they have turned his choices for press secretaries and different cabinet positions into punching bags.

In this way, the modern-day comedians have used their influential platform that reaches millions of Americans to support a liberal political line, and they have contributed to the divisive political climate in America with their snide remarks. In many societies today, such commentary might be shut down as damaging to the social order, and the comedians might even be jailed for mocking their political leaders. But in the U.S. such commentary is permitted under the guise of free speech. Yet, there are limits, such as the classic example of someone yelling "fire" in a crowded theater, leading to a stampede to get out that could even lead to the death of some patrons. Right now, the comedians are free to say what they want, but they could go over the line of what should be permitted. An example could be joking about the threats made to the President or his family members, which could be taken by someone who is mentally disturbed as a call to take action to carry out the threat.

Still another concern is that the vast majority of political comedians tend to lean left, as pointed out by Patrick Bromley in "The Top Political Comedians in America", posted March 29, 2018 on ThoughtCo.com. So collectively, these comedians are using their position to influence many millions of voters, especially when a similar message is reinforced on different shows, such as if one listens to the reaction of Stephen Colbert, Trevor Noah, Seth Myers, and the Saturday Night Live crew to the news of the day. The focus of the monologues, guests, and sketches are almost always about President Trump and others supporting his administration, and they point to what's wrong, which can contribute to undermining faith in our institutions. While the comedians' defense is they are using free speech to be funny, they are also using humor to support the liberal political agenda, so they largely don't feature any foibles of the liberal political leaders.

In turn, their comedy can influence the way we vote, as Evan Fleischer points out in an October 2016 article in *The Guardian:* "Can Late-Night TV Hosts Influence the Way We Vote?" Though Fleischer was asking the question before the results came in for the 2016 election, he pointed out that "Over the past few years, late-night comedy has been taken far more seriously than in the days when Johnny Carson was host." He also cited an *Atlantic* article which observed that "comedians have taken on the role of public intellectuals."

In fact, in some of these "comedy" sketches, the talk show hosts are often "making earnest, quite un-funny political pleas" to cite a July 2018 article by Olivia Goldhill on Quaritzy: "'Nanette' and Why a New Wave of Comedians Don't Want to Be Funny." As Goldhill notes: "More and more comedians are losing the jokes part altogether. Having become political comedians, they're dropping the comedy act and becoming straightforward commentators."

And it gets worse, according to an article by Noel Murray on *TheWeek* website: "Why Political Comedians Will Always Let You Down." As the article points out, a big problem is the comedians can do anything for a laugh, so a funny comment can have the ring of truth, but it doesn't have to be fully truthful. The popular political comics such as Stephen Colbert, Seth Myers, John Oliver, Samantha Bee, and the *Saturday Night Live* anchors can be quite funny when they point up the failures of our modern institutions. But, as Murray points out, they don't always get everything right. In fact, they may not be able to do so in the minutes or even seconds they have to make their point."

Then, too, in the comedians' one-sided approach to making fun of our institutions, they focus on attacking President Trump and his administration. But they don't go after the opposing side. Accordingly, we have to recognize the comedians of the airwaves for the one-sided view of the world they present. And we have to realize that under the cover of humor, their attacks can be very influential. They could even motivate dangerous individuals to take action against the Trump administration.

So what can be done? Advertisers might boycott such shows or their networks. Another approach might be to create a commission to create guidelines for what comedians can do or not do when they are engaged in political humor. The commission could then seek public support for its guidelines in order to influence the comedians to keep their acts within acceptable bounds. Otherwise, they might suffer widespread criticism for their comedy and even a career meltdown, such as happened when Kathy Griffin held up a bloody head of Trump and lost most of her future appearances, as a result.

PART 8: USING A SOCIAL MEDIA AND VIDEO CAMPAIGN TO HELP FIX THE CRIMINAL JUSTICE SYSTEM

CHAPTER 26: CRIMINAL JUSTICE EXPERT TURNS SOCIAL MEDIA CAMPAIGN ON REDUCING CRIME INTO A BOOK

Crime in America in a Nutshell

Highlights from *Crime in America*
as Seen in the Social Media

by Paul Brakke

FOR IMMEDIATE RELEASE

Can a book and social media campaign to fix the criminal justice system lead to social and political change and new approaches to reduce crime? That's what I have sought to do by turning a 6-month social media campaign on fixing the system into a book. Additionally, I have used the book to suggest fixes for the opioid crisis and immigration mess.

This campaign is featured in the book *Crime in America in a Nutshell: Highlights from Crime in America as Seen in the Social Media* from American Leadership Books. In both the campaign and the book, I describe new ways for criminal justice reform from a conservative perspective. The goal is to point up what's wrong and find ways to fix a costly inefficient system that creates more criminals. *Crime in America in a Nutshell* brings together all of the social media posts which feature highlights from *Crime in America* along with photos and videos. So the new book quickly features the most important facts and recommendations on fixing this very troubled system.

To get out this important message, I have made the *Nutshell* book permanently free, so it's like finding a treasure map that leads readers to the more in-depth *Crime in America,* which details the facts and careful analysis leading to these recommendations. *Crime in America* is a synthesis of six comprehensive books written for law-enforcement professionals, academics, legislators, and social service providers. Besides writing some books for general readers, I have been using others to reach out to members of Congress, criminal justice professionals, and organizations concerned with crime to recommend new and better ways to combat crime and create a more effective and responsive criminal justice system.

To achieve these ends, I have created a three-step program to get out my message about the problems faced by anyone dealing with crime and criminal justice in America:

1) a social media campaign on reducing crime and fixing the criminal justice system, and a book based on this campaign: *Crime in American in a Nutshell*;

2) a general interest book about ways to reduce crime and fix the system: *Crime in America: Conservatives' Approaches to Criminals, Police, Crime, and the Opioid Crisis*

3) six generally more comprehensive books about how to fix the problems with the police, courts, and prisons, as well as deal with the opioid crisis and illegal immigration.

My conservative approach to crime and criminal justice is unique, since usually liberals discuss ways to reform the system through more of a social welfare approach. By contrast, I advocate reducing costs through reducing crime, recidivism, and incarceration rates. I recommend doing this by turning ex-cons into more productive citizens, strengthening ex-con's families, and using treatment instead of long sentences for prisoners who have committed less serious non-violent crimes, especially prisoners who are older or mentally ill. I have used Department of Justice crime statistics and comparisons with programs that have worked in different countries to make my case.

CHAPTER 27: VIDEO CAMPAIGN ON BETTER RELATIONSHIP WITH COPS AND FIXING THE CRIMINAL JUSTICE SYSTEM, BASED ON NEW BOOK

Can a video campaign to promote citizen-police relationships, reduce crime, and fix the criminal justice system lead to social and political change? That's been my goal in conducting a 6-month video and social media campaign based on my latest book: *Crime in America.*

To this end, I have been turning chapters in the book into short videos to spread the book's message more widely. Additionally, I created a book featuring all of my social media campaigns for 6 months. It's called *Crime in America in a Nutshell: Highlights from Crime in America as Seen in the Social Media.*

I have developed this four way approach -- through the videos, social media postings, book of these postings, and the original *Crime in America* book -- to bring about criminal justice reform from a conservative perspective. I consider the First Step sentencing reform bill a good beginning for the reform process, but I believe that so much more needs to be done, as described in my videos, postings, and books.

The last videos in the series deal with improving citizen-police relationships based on a chapter in *Crime in America*. The videos feature a number of topics -- the effects of protests against the police in black communities, the need for a national clearinghouse for citizen-police review reports, and the need to stop the media from sensationalizing stories that are fueling racial anger. Other recommendations in these videos are providing more police training on community awareness and removing restrictions on filming the police without inferring on police duties. A previous series of videos offered suggestions for healing the divisions in U.S. society.

The *Crime in America* book on which these videos are based is a synthesis of six comprehensive books written for law enforcement professionals, academics, legislators, and social service providers. Besides writing this book for general readers, I have been using these books to reach out to members of Congress, criminal justice professionals, and organizations concerned with crime in order to recommend new and better ways to combat crime and create a more effective and responsive criminal justice system.

My conservative approach to crime and criminal justice is unique, since usually liberals discuss ways to reform the system through more of a social welfare approach. These suggested reforms deal with everything from making changes in the police and courts to the jails and prisons. I have been using Department of Justice crime statistics and comparisons with programs that have worked in different countries and U.S. cities to make this case for reform.

CHAPTER 28: CONTINUED VIDEO CAMPAIGN ON COPS, PRISONS, AND DIVISIONS IN AMERICA

Given the power of video, I have had a video campaign produced based on chapters in my latest book, *Crime in America,* published by American Leadership Books. The videos recommend new ways to improve relationships with the police; reduce costs, incarceration rates, and crime with better prison policies and more community treatment programs; and heal the many divisions in American society. The videos also provide an entry to the more in-depth book chapters designed to help citizens better understand what to do, so they can help to influence legislators through local groups and their votes.

I recently combined the insights from these videos into a 6-month social media campaign which is featured in a new book called *Crime in America in a Nutshell: Highlights from Crime in America as Seen in the Social Media.* The video campaign, social media postings, and book are all designed to bring the message of criminal justice reform from a conservative perspective to a broad audience.

As part of this campaign, I have been reaching out to legislators and governors to consult with them on the best approaches to criminal justice reform in their jurisdiction. I strongly believe we need to make changes based on current data about what works and doesn't. We should learn from other countries, too -- especially about the more effective prison policies in countries like Germany, Sweden, and Norway. They emphasize rehabilitation, shorter sentences, and getting ex-cons who have committed less serious crimes back into the community, so they can unite with their families and become more productive citizens.

We also need to be more understanding of the difficulties police face, such as shown in my videos on these key topics:
- the effects of the protests against the police in black communities,
- the need to stop the media from sensationalizing stories that are fueling racial anger,
- the benefits of providing more community awareness training for police.

Other videos based on the book deal with the opioid crisis and illegal immigration, and with finding ways to create safer communities with less conflict between different groups in society based on race, ethnicity, income, and other differences.

A key message of this and other books and videos from American Leadership Books and the campaigns based on them is that we have to find ways to better work together. Also, we need to find ways to fix the inequalities and injustices throughout the criminal justice system, from the police and courts to the prisons. Individual citizens can play a role through their votes and their input at local community meetings. But we also need to reach out to Federal and state government officials, politicians, and the media to join together to make some of these recommended changes. I have sought to use my books and these campaigns to help educate these officials and media professionals on the changes we so desperately need.

WANT TO KNOW MORE?

To learn more, you can get a free *Crime in America in a Nutshell,* as well as a free review copy of *Crime in America* or *Fractured America.* I am offering *Crime in America in a Nutshell* for free to anyone who wants to see the highlights of this social media campaign, as well as review copies of *Crime in America* and *Fractured America.* In addition, copies are available for government officials who might incorporate into legislation some of my suggested ways to reduce crime and fix the criminal justice system. Members of the media are also invited to request copies of the books.

As part of my social media campaign, I have had over 70 videos created that highlight the main points of my approach to reducing crime and reforming the system. One of the most recent videos is "Want to Know More about U.S. Crime?" https://youtu.be/qkZkXwjsEzc.

So far, as a result of my extensive research on crime, the criminal justice system and the divisions in American society, I have authored eight books on criminal justice as the publisher of American Leadership Books, which specializes in this subject. Six of the books deal with what to do about crime in America and one focuses on understanding and healing the great national divides in America. These books include: *Fixing the U.S. Criminal Justice System, The Price of Justice in America,* and *The Costly U.S. Prison System,* which were written primarily for law enforcement professionals, government officials, and academics, and *Fractured America* written for a more general audience.

If you want to know more about the topics covered in Parts 4 and 5 of *Uncertain Justice,* you can read and review *Fractured America.*

Copies of *Crime in America* and *Fractured America* for review are available to the general public at no charge at www.crimeinamericathebook.com. A free copy of *Crime in America in a Nutshell* is available on Kindle or for a free PDF, epub, or mobi book, go to www.crimeinamericapublishing.com.

Both *Crime in America* and *Fractured America* are also available as audiobooks.

For media copies of the book, more information on American Leadership Books, and myself, or to set up interviews, please contact my publicist Jana Collins of Jones O'Malley at jana@jonesomalley.com or call 818-762-8353.

GET A FREE REVIEW COPY

IF YOU WANT TO REVIEW CRIME IN AMERICA

Discover this powerful new book. It's all about crime, the police, criminal justice, and the opioid crisis.

Get a FREE review copy. Agree to review *Crime in America* and you'll get a FREE copy of a $14.95 paperback and $3.99 e-book as PDF, epub, or mobi file.

Learn about our new books and win unique prizes!

You'll get a FREE copy in a PDF, epub, or mobi format.

You'll also be the first to learn about our new books and have an opportunity to win unique prizes!

SEND ME MY REVIEW COPY
(www.crimeinamericapublishing.com)

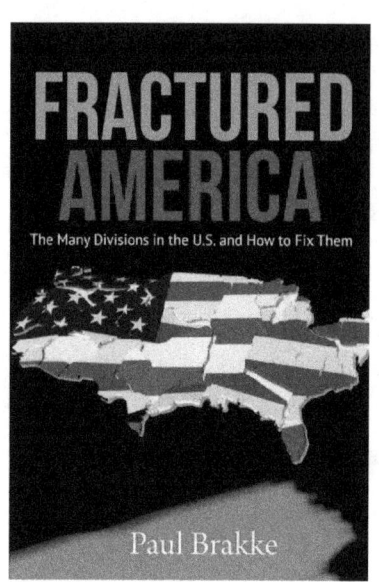

ABOUT THE AUTHOR

Paul Brakke is a scientist based in the Little Rock, Arkansas area. He became interested in studying the criminal justice system because, as described in his first book *American Justice?*, his life was turned upside down by the system.

He has previously told his wife's story along with a critique of the criminal justice system in *American Justice?* After that, Brakke went on to look at other problems in the system and the country in general and how to fix them.

His other books include: *Crime in America, Fractured America, The Costly U.S. Prison System, Fixing the U.S. Criminal Justice System, Dealing with Illegal Immigration and the Opioid Crisis, The Price of Justice in America,* and *Cops Aren't Such Bad Guys*. To publish them, he set up a publishing company American Leadership Books, featuring books on criminal justice and social issues, which are available in print and e-books through Amazon, Ingram, Kindle, and other major distributors. Since these first books were directed primarily at law enforcement professionals, politicians, and academics, Brakke is now developing a series of books on criminal justice to appeal to the general public, especially to conservatives.

The books' website is: www.americanleadershipbooks.com.

Audiobooks are available at: https://www.audible.com/author/Paul-Brakke/B0714KG374

OTHER AVAILABLE BOOKS

Crime in America

Fractured America

Fixing the U.S. Criminal Justice System

The Price of Justice in America

The Costly U.S. Prison System

Cops Aren't Such Bad Guys

CONTACT US

For more information:

AMERICAN LEADERSHIP BOOKS
8 Portia Drive
Little Rock, Arkansas 72212
brakkep@gmail.com

CPSIA information can be obtained
at www.ICGtesting.com
Printed in the USA
BVHW041616080419
544933BV00009B/36/P